Halcyon Days

JAG Beard

Happy Birthday Mike.
Best Wishes
Gordon

Produced by Holborn House Ltd October 2014.
Holborn House, Brains Green, Blakeney, GL15 4AJ

A young boy's life in the Gloucestershire village of Lydbrook 1930-1943

Herewith a few musings on a lad's life pre-war in a Gloucestershire Village.

For Yasmin, Oliver, Douglas and Francesca.

Acknowledgements

My thanks to Fiona Rogers, Oliver and Paul Beard my computer guru, without whose expertise and advice this epistle would never have seen daylight, and Mark Lodge of WBML publishing for proof reading. Also Terence Ward for his help and advice when confirmation of events was needed.

The author was born and bred in Gloucestershire whence, after service in the Fleet Air Arm he returned to civilian life to commence work and study Engineering.

He became a Chartered engineer, going into teaching and eventually ending his career as a Senior Lecturer. He lives at present at Ross-on-Wye, Herefordshire

Contents

Chapter 1 Our Valley

We sat looking out over the valley as we did quite often on Summer weekends or at holiday time, when the sun shone and everything was well with our world, which was mainly when we could get away unscathed from home and the errands which might need running, if possible with a jam sandwich or a piece of cake if we were lucky, in our hand or an old pair of binoculars belonging to my father, which dated back to the first world war. We weren't sure which was more important, the jam sandwich or the views through the glasses, but we enjoyed both you may be sure, and while the sandwich held no surprises, sometimes the views did, for we soon realised that if you sat still, you became invisible to many of those engaged in nefarious doings over a whole range of activities, all of which required a furtive manner, and whilst we might have mentioned what we had seen if they were possibly criminal acts, there were others which were mainly of interest, which to us was anything which moved, particularly if it was something involving two people of opposite gender.

From our viewpoint we saw small fields sloping down to the valley floor, with the sun chasing cloud shadows across them, populated with the occasional sheep or cow. Banks of trees grew at the steepest parts where fields couldn't be made, while other valley slopes were covered by the green of bracken and the occasional small tree. There was one field in particular which excited our imagination. It had a small ruined cottage in it, from which, it was said, a secret passage ran to a local pub called the Anchor, for someone to escape by, but from whom and why, we didn't know. While we treated this with some caution, the pub had in it a room used as an outhouse and which according to the publican was called "the jud 'ouse" in the vernacular, or the dead house, and which during the civil war was apparently piled high with dead bodies of men killed in some local skirmish. There appeared to be little evidence of this fight, but the story suited us and provided colour for visitors, indeed it is still mentioned to this day in that pub, although the said pub wasn't even opened until the early 19th century, but we didn't know that, and neither do the visitors.

The sides of the valley were precipitous in places and in one part a footpath was hacked out in steps for people to use, being known as Jacob's ladder, and whilst it could not to be said to lead to heaven it probably sent a few folks there before their time. One local baker employed donkeys to carry loaves, packed into panniers, up it to his customers, and those donkeys were the fittest creatures in the county.

Immediately below our perch ran a single track railway line which had been carved out of the valley side and carried a steam driven engine which drew trucks of coal from the local mines, and the occasional passenger carriage, and which was, of course, a constant source of fascination to us lads as it puffed and wheezed it's way to its destination with the main line some mile or so away. During its journey it passed over a viaduct which stretched from one side of the valley to the other, this being a source of excitement and sheer terror, as to ride over it gave the feeling that you were floating in the air like a butterfly and would fall to the ground at any minute. The engine also showed an interest in the chickens belonging to a rather eccentric villager who lived a few yards from the rails, and ran over any it could get its wheels at, thus prompting the said villager, it was said, and believed by some, to nail a train timetable in the chicken pen to let them know when the next train was due, and save them from meeting the great cockerel in the sky prematurely. While we didn't believe this, we always tended to hurry past this particular cottage, which was also, by a strange coincidence, the one in which I first saw the light of day. I wonder. But my parents seemed eminently sensible however.

Our valley playground was, in fact, some two miles in length, at its widest a mile, shaped like an hourglass with a strong steam running down its length, emptying into the river Wye, and at its narrowest, a chasm 200 yards wide, with precipitous sides covered in trees. Our observation point was a spur of rock which jutted out some 300 feet above the valley floor, this latter having the only road running along it.

This road had a couple of spurs feeding small collections of houses leading off it but, in the main, the villagers cottages dotted the sides of the valley, seemingly at random, many built illegally, as they were on land belonging to the Crown and had been built by the time honoured method of encroachment and indeed, in earlier times many were cleared by the authorities, but the people had returned over the years. They looked as though thrown there by a giant hand, having small lanes or paths made by their occupants down to the valley floor or to the nearest road spur, which was great for us lads when dashing about this network of pathways.

The stream running through our valley was the thing which gave it life, in that it was used to provide power for industry from Roman times, but some people might also say it brought about its death, because when industry came in, Nature died, or, at least, was made rather sickly. But to us it was something to try and jump over and sail sticks down in competition to see whose was fastest. It was also the local sewer, and in later years I often wondered whether we only missed typhoid or dysentery, or some other dread disease by default. But it may be that some of us didn't.

Throughout the centuries there was little in the way of people living here, except perhaps the odd charcoal burner or men digging out iron ore, as this was part of the forest lands designated by the Normans as their playground, being well populated with wild boar and therefore to be kept clear of Saxons or any form of rabble, but from early times it was known that iron ore lay beneath the surrounding hills and, with timber and water power available it was inevitable that iron working would become a major industry here. From the early 17th century various men were given permission to set up iron foundries and, in the earlier years of the 20th Century the firm of Richard Thomas and Baldwin set up a factory to manufacture tin-plate here, and proceeded to dam the stream in places to create large ponds, set up waterwheels and forges and all the buildings and machinery which went with it, while a coal mine named the Arthur and Edward colliery was active, together with a firm making electric cables and there were various other small industries.

All this activity brought in people, including us, but, of course it ruined the valley, but, by the early 1930's the tin-plate industry had gone to a town nearby, which meant that the workmen now had to travel to get work there, and I recollect seeing groups of them standing, waiting for rickety old buses with their enamel tea cans and their food in cloth bags, dressed in rough working clothes, looking somehow sad to us, as though they were going somewhere and not coming back. What was left behind was heaps of spoil, derelict buildings and a desolate landscape which nature was trying it's best to cover up with bushes, small trees covered with creepers, and grass. A lesson in what human greed can accomplish when it tries.

While this industry was taking place in the lower end of the valley, the upper end had its coal mine which scattered its slag, apparently where it liked. Thus a huge slag tip of 30,000 tons of blue waste was deposited in its centre and, while providing somewhere for us lads to run over, was also an eyesore.

Then, someone, somewhere, sometime had a brilliant idea. *Let's move it.* That someone was no-one else but our school headmaster Mr. Sidney Miles. The time was July 1934, when a meeting was called to consider what could be done. The outcome was that this gentleman, together with three other local men became the nucleus of a great enterprise - to make us a playing field, and it certainly made a difference to our young lives. I sometimes think that if these men had lived today they would have been awarded at least an OBE or something similar, but, as it was they received nothing but the unspoken thanks of us children and the village at large. This was in the early 1930's when millionaires were rather thin on the ground, at least in our village, and a playing field where we could kick a football or play a game of tennis was way beyond our hopes or expectations.

But, suddenly, metal tubs on four wheels, usually used to carry coal appeared, as did lengths of iron rails, and it was assumed that the local colliery had donated them, and so the work started, and us lads, like many another, watched these men whose faces were familiar to us, slogging away in rain and shine, an old sack slung over the shoulders to keep off the worst of the rain, but still working, and perhaps wondered why they would work like this for us youngsters. I don't suppose anyone asked them.

This was a monumental voluntary effort by the local men, some 300 of them, many of them being out-of-work miners, who cleared the waste by hand, and I sometimes wonder if they had the credit they deserved for their efforts. Still, in 1936 the foundation stone for the project was laid by the

11

Duke of Kent, and as a small boy I stood with mother on a rainy day to see the great man bang a stone with a gavel and formally declare it nearly finished. Having finished doing the stone a serious mischief, he jumped in his car and amid much tugging of the forelock, disappeared, no doubt to take sherry with the Lord Lieutenant of the County but it was decent of him to call and cheer on the peasantry, and it gave us all something to talk about. There were, of course, the local dignitaries gathered to be seen, who wouldn't know a shovel or pickaxe even if they fell over them, but we didn't care, and I don't suppose the men who had worked bothered much either. We now had an official playground.

But that was not all, for, as though a fairy had waved a magic wand, appeared swings, slides, boat like contraptions which swung up and down, rotating cones which also swung up and down, and other likewise lethal playground attractions which appeared to be clothed by dozens of children, all screaming and fighting, all shoving and pushing to be the next to jump aboard and risk death or amputation, or at least a serious injury. But oddly enough this didn't happen, which says a great deal for our sense of self preservation, and nimbleness of foot. Who paid for this equipment we never knew, only that they were a new phenomenon to be exploited.

But, as with most new attractions, it wasn't long before we became tired of swings and slides and were back with our own gangs doing our usual things, but this was a good time, and looking back we should have been more appreciative of what was offered by these local people.

Some of the men who helped to move the "Blue Mound".
Grandfather Ward is on the right.

The valley then was a source of endless pleasure, and we knew who lived where, the hedgerows which had the best nut trees, where to pick the largest and juiciest blackberries and elderberries for making wine and pies, where tadpoles could be found in season to take to school in jam jars to watch change into frogs (we never actually saw the final transition, as they suddenly disappeared, no doubt with

13

the connivance of the teacher), whose orchard had the best apples, and the whereabouts of every conker and chestnut tree within a three mile radius.

The picking of the above blackberries was quite an event as some local women picked and sold them for cash, which, of course they found most useful. For this to be a viable proposition however, a considerable quantity of berries had to be picked.

A local man had a large piece of ground high on a ridge at the edge of the village which was of little use and was virtually wasteland. This was because the subsoil was poor and would grow very little of any use due to the mining of iron ore in earlier times. What it did grow, however, was blackberry bushes in great quantity.

This was just what was needed, and whole families could be seen, (at least the mothers and children), climbing the hill, laden with baskets, buckets and even baths and then dispersing into the bushes like flocks of multi-coloured birds to get to the picking.

When all the receptacles were full, the results would be carried to the centre of the village, where a lorry, complete with a large weighing machine, would be waiting, attended by a man who tended to wear a brown coat as favoured by warehousemen, breeches and highly polished gaiters and boots, topped off with a brown derby. I seem to remember his name was Brown too.

After weighing, the women were paid off, and the man in the brown gaiters would drive off with his cargo of glistening berries, to be made into jam we assumed. This activity was hard work for the women but for many it was a case of "when the Devil drives---"

The hands of the women and the lips of the children were, of course, always stained with berry juice, and a new arrival from outer space would have been forgiven if they concluded that ancient Britons were alive and well and painting themselves with blue woad.

Whilst the picking of blackberries may have suited some, we preferred the collection of elderberries. We would be given baskets and walking sticks to bend down the high branches of the bushes, and sent off to pick the sprays of shining berries. This was far more fun for lads as it also enabled us to pick hazel nuts at the same time, so with pockets full of nuts and baskets full of berries a good time was had by all.

The contents of our baskets was conveyed home in triumph and while we were sent out for more, the womenfolk shredded the berries from the stalks with forks, put them into a large copper bowl usually used for doing the washing, and got on with the winemaking. This ruby red liquor was known as the poor man's port wine, and although we weren't allowed to try it, the rest of the family seemed to enjoy it, although I can never remember seeing any of them under the influence.

The making of wine from all sorts of fruit and vegetables was, of course, common in all parts of the country, as wines made from grapes was unaffordable to the man in the street. While a glass or two was perhaps indulged in in the winter time when something was needed to warm the cockles of the heart, so to speak, it was at Christmas time I remember it best. But more later...

It was, above all *our* valley, not a place to be ignored, vibrant with energy and colour and life, a place just made for boys like us, now, alas, mostly gone.

Chapter 2 Our Village

Our valley, our village, was a lively, living place, with a range of shops from butchers, one a Mr. Mann who epitomised the butcher with his large size and happy red face, a second by the name of Horace Brain who was elderly, slim and who wore a white coat, a blue and white striped apron and a straw boater. One of the old school, whose shop was immaculate but which had sawdust on the floor, to one selling hardware, to two grocers, three bakers, a post office, a chemist who handed out pills and advice and was consulted far more frequently that the local doctor, probably because if the doctor was consulted, one had to pay, unless you were on the panel, as it was called, whereby you paid a given amount every week and then had your treatment free. There was more ill health than was necessary in those days and what a good thing it is that we now have the National Health Service and what a great man was Aneurin Bevan, the man who proposed that treatment for illness should be free at the point of delivery.

There were also sundry sweetshops, greengrocers, two garages, two hairdressers, (one ladies, one gents), a business which manufactured lemonade and soft drinks from a very pure spring in the centre of the village, some seven well patronised public houses, a coal merchant, and a very small building which housed a fish and chip shop, the owner being one Curly Jones (the curly being a nickname). How this business managed to exist we never knew, but there were always queues to get in and we were always on hand to get the cooked batter which came off the fish, and which he would put in a cone of paper and give to us urchins. There was even a branch of Lloyds bank which opened a couple of days a week. The person who worked there must have almost died of boredom as no-one had any money at that time.

Of the bakers I had a personal relationship, in that one belonged to an uncle, and which became a very large one in later years, and one to the father-in-law of another uncle and this one was my favourite as on Saturday mornings I was allowed to sit in the warmth of the bakehouse and watch the fresh bread being taken out of the oven, ready for the morning deliveries. I can still smell that bread even today.

His oven was fired with wood which had been trimmed off trees at the wood yard, and this seemed to give some added taste to the bread. The bread was delivered by horse and cart, by his two daughters, and I was allowed to fetch and ride on the horse from the orchard where he lived, and dreamed his dreams of cantering home in first place in the Grand National, then sit in state on the cart whilst my aunts did their deliveries. Even Boadicea in her chariot couldn't have been prouder. The bread was packed in the back of the cart on, and covered by, flour sacks to keep them away from the weather, and on one never to be forgotten morning I leaned back too far, tipped over backwards and ended up with a very red face amongst the bread. It must be said that the ladies had a fine range of swear words.

The man's hairdresser was really a barber and styling was something only dreamed about, but on Saturday mornings his shop was also the meeting place of many of the local men, who were there to gossip, and discuss the rights and wrongs of the local football team's selection for the afternoon match. It was also the place where many men, usually more elderly, came for their weekly shave. They would go puffing in, with a face full of white bristles and emerge with a shiny, very red face from the superheated towels applied by the barber, almost unrecognisable but with a definite resemblance to a well-polished billiards ball.

There was a story that the local vicar went in for a shave one

17

day, and the barber, as usual, lathered him up then walked behind him to shave under his chin, at which point the vicar leapt out of the chair and instructed the barber to shave him from the front or not at all. He must have thought he was about to cut his throat, perhaps having taken umbrage at something he had said in one of his sermons. Heaven knows, but he wasn't that bad a churchman.

Of course, when the barber was called up at the outbreak of war, the lads had to go the ladies hairdresser for a haircut, which seemed very odd, but we soon got used to it, and to the smelly lotion they applied when finished with addressing our waves and quiffs, but some of the comments our mates made were not true at all.

There wasn't always a chemist in the village, and prior to his arrival there was but one doctor to administer to the people's medical problems. Of course, the less we knew him the better we liked him, but he was said to be good, although I had my doubts when he sewed up a gash on my eyebrow with what appeared to be very thick cat gut. He was not my favourite person that day.

As well as doing everything else, he was his own pharmacist, and appeared to have a particular liking for large brown demijohns filled with some concoction or other which was his favourite medicine for all sorts of conditions, from the common cold to typhoid fever. But whatever we suffered with seemed to improve after a bottle or two of this elixir, so he obviously knew what he was talking about.

Thinking about peoples' health generally, I think that we were healthier then than we are now perhaps because we had less chemicals in our food and life was simpler, or that people were tougher, and got on with life, ill or not.

Although many folk had their interests, such as amateur theatre, gardening, sports etc., it was music which claimed the greatest following. This wasn't peculiar to our village as in those days every village had its male voice choir, and many, a brass band. This was, perhaps partly due to our close proximity to Wales, with their musical tradition, and the feeling for music perhaps came to us by some kind of osmosis.

The villages often competed with each other in friendly rivalry, and contests which were held outdoors in summer, with sometimes six or more bands marching through the village, being judged as they marched, and then again on the field where the completion was held. The choirs too sang on a stage outdoors, with the judges sitting in a closed tent so that they could not see, at least in theory, who was performing. Many were the mutterings that it was all a fiddle could be heard, but the same thing happened every year, so people must have enjoyed it. The beer tent did very well too.

As my father was a member of our village choir I would sometimes creep into the local hall where they met for rehearsals to watch Mr. Evans the choir master trying to get the best out of a piece of music, and the love of the sound of a male voice choir is with me still.

Altogether the village was alive and people talked to one another and cared about each other, whereas today the people have left to live in every part of the country, and the old bonds have gone. Now, people don't even know their neighbours.

I returned to the village recently, and left it feeling profoundly depressed, as it was no longer our village but somewhere alien, the shops and older houses gone to be replaced by modern boxes, perhaps more comfortable to live in but not as picturesque as the older ones. Small businesses had disappeared as had the people. A dead or dying village.

But maybe I am wrong. Maybe there is still life there. I hope so.

Chapter 3 The School

I suppose it all started at about 8.45am on a morning in early September in the year 1931, when my Mother stood holding my hand at the school gate. I say suppose because I really can't remember exactly what happened being so young, but I do remember looking up at other Mothers towering above me, all with children in hand and swathed in shawls supporting more offspring on their hips in Welsh fashion.

I can still almost feel the terror mixed with excitement as I stood before that closed gate whose bars seemed three inches in diameter, waiting for the teacher to let us in. I was hopping from foot to foot, probably wanting to go to the toilet, but still proud of a new cap and new short trousers which I was wearing for the first time. I was also clutching a brown paper bag containing an apple which, Mother had impressed upon me, was to be eaten at playtime and not before, as I would be going home for lunch. Perhaps my parents had prepared me for this momentous change but, whatever the case, I know I wanted to go to this place where some of my cousins were, and where, according to everyone else, this was the place to be.

At last someone arrived, and in I went, without a thought for my poor Mother who had just given up her offspring to the world, to start my exploration of the world of knowledge, although little did I know then, how many years later I would realise that I had only scratched the surface of what was there before me.

The building was red brick with nothing to commend it in terms of aesthetic value, the infants school being separate from the big school, the whole thing surrounded by playgrounds and a large school garden, of which more later, but it was new to us and seemed enormous. In fact it was a small school with about 250 children in total between the ages of 4/5 and 14 years, and on that morning there were about 30 new pupils, the vast majority being strangers to one another.

Our teacher during that first year was a Miss Peggy Wheatstone, and I can still see her giving instructions on making some small object to take home for our doting parents, usually something involving paper and paste which was applied with gay abandon with a brush, officially to the paper, but more often to ourselves and anything or anybody within reach. She was thin and pale with mousey hair, and tended to wear a lot of brown in her dress, sensible shoes, and thick brown stockings and, if she could hear me now, would I am sure, agree that she was rather plain. But, to us, she was a cross between the Archangel Gabriel and God, who could do no wrong. She was the fount of all knowledge and while, no doubt, our parents were fed up with Miss said this, and Miss said that, that's the cross that teachers of infants have to bear I suppose. She must have had a really rough time, with a mob of children, some frightened, others worldly wise, but all of them wanting something. She was not a trained teacher, but rather some nebulous classroom assistant grade and I'm sure she was sent to look after us as some sort of punishment for past misdemeanours.

That first year was like being let loose in some sort of fairyland. We played with sand, bricks, painted animals and people in multi-coloured poster paints, in shapes unknown to science, and started writing in very large letters with chalk on slates etc. But whatever the joys of that time, the most important thing that happened to us was that we had started to have relationships with all these other lads and girls, disliking some and liking others, these likes and dislikes staying with us right through our school days.

Playtime was the melting pot when we were turned loose to run off the energy untapped by sitting still, or at least, confined, for an hour or two. It lasted for about 10 minutes, and it was here that friendships were made, and little groups started to come together, from which some children were rejected, and others admitted and was, perhaps, the most formative time in our lives, as these concepts had, until now, been foreign to us and needed to be understood and endured for good or ill. Anyway, the first year ended and battle hardened and thicker skinned we moved on to greater things.

We now thought that we knew all about everything and that life was marvellous and a never ending delight, but then followed Class Two, a classroom ruled by Mrs. Ella Wilce, a lady of middle age, who left me with the impression that she wore a lot of black with white lace collars, and everything about her immaculate. She was our first introduction to education proper when we were made to realise that we were in this building for something other than playing, such as reading, writing with pencils, and finding out that two plus two equalled four, and, looking back I realise that here was *discipline* wielded with the panache and dedication of Genghis Khan, a rude awakening to us all. In fact I can't remember any of us putting a foot out of line as she seemed able to look around corners and read every thought in our heads before we had it. But this time passed swiftly and we gradually left babyhood behind and became lads and girls, with all that implied.

But now we had arrived at another traumatic turning point in our young lives, the move to Big School and away from the Infants playground and into new relationships with bigger children, who made sure that we should consider ourselves as being entirely inferior and to be ignored whenever possible.

This didn't bother us however and we just went our own way and played our own games, and, although there was a certain amount of mild bullying, it was at least general and not directed at individuals. Except for one of the bigger boys who seemed to take an occasional swipe whenever within arm's length, and the recipient was smaller than him, and one or two others who delighted in putting any younger ones they could catch into the basement of the boiler room which was protected by a tall railing and called the lion's den. Here we would languish until it was time to go back into class, with an occasional attempt to get out, but all in all we knew that this was one war we were not going to win until we had sufficient allies, and so put up with it without too much concern, and waited for our turn to be the jailer.

I was lucky in that although I was a single child, my Mother being unable, or unwilling, to take another chance, I had a big cousin called Cyril who I could always rely on to drag me out from under a pile of bodies trying to scrag one another. I thought a lot of Cyril and when, many years later, he served in the Royal Navy on the Russian convoys, I looked upon his round red face and quiet grin topped with his round sailors cap, with pride and not a little awe.

Here we found a new world of marvellous and frightening sensations, from a small and dusty museum full of objects collected during somebody's travels, such as a dried seahorse, or a sprig of coral, to a visit from the school dentist, where a long line of children would be found standing in a corridor, waiting to have their teeth looked over, many girls weeping and lads trying to be very brave, waiting to be sat in a chair and suffer the extraction of teeth. These so-called dentists had much to answer for and their motto should have been "Have 'em in and get 'em out". One of the bigger lads became the hero of the hour when he severely bit the finger of one of the sadists, causing the torture chamber to be closed for the rest of the day. Good for George.

The first two years in our new environment passed quickly and pleasantly, firstly under the control of Miss Edith Preece, a pretty woman who endeared herself to us lads by marrying Bill Hale the goalkeeper of the local football team, and then Miss Evelyn Walding, a quiet person, but capable of applying a ruler to the knuckles when necessary. Our days were filled with learning our tables, first steps in writing and all the other exciting things we were called upon to sample; especially if chosen to be milk monitor and go and fetch the milk for morning break (this half pint of milk being provided free to all children by the government of the day, to help prevent illnesses such as rickets, etc.).

It should be remembered here, that the time was the early thirties when the economy was on the rocks, many men could not find work, and children in many cases came to school hungry and badly clothed against inclement weather. What an outrage it is that this condition still pertains to this day in many schools. Many parents of the older boys took the view that footwear should be boots which were indestructible, with metal tips on heel and toe and the rest of the sole covered in studs, and this, therefore, was what the rest of us yearned for, particularly as the studs were necessary for making sparks on the roads. But, in general, parents did their best to send their children to school decently clad even if jackets or dresses were hand-me-downs, or the seat of the trouser was patched.

The third year saw us with Miss Dunn, a young woman who stood no nonsense and who took us for what might laughingly be called gym. This consisted standing in rows in the playground and waving our arms and legs around to her instruction. The playground could not be described as the playing fields of Eton, and I doubt if many battles would be likely to be won on that slab of asphalt except for the ones between ourselves. This meant that she was fit and capable, we reckoned, of taking on a full on charge by a maddened buffalo and stopping it dead. On one occasion a lad who should have known better, caused her some annoyance and the conversation which followed was something like this:

"Owen, leave the room and go and see Mr. Miles"

"Don't want to Miss"

"Owen, do as you're told"

"Shan't Miss"

"Owen, if you don't go *now* I shall remove you"

This was fighting talk all round and the class were ready and willing to cheer on their own personal favourite. However, without turning a hair she simply removed him bodily, desk and all, which impressed us no end. A lady of great determination and spirit it must be said.

As a group of lads we were a fairly carefree bunch but it was 1939 and other things thrust themselves on our attention, not least the outbreak of war. Everything was now excitement, and new happenings and the last thing we thought about was school, but we still had to turn up, but as soon as we could, we were out and about; all eyes, ears, hopes and fears.

Gas masks.

We arrived that year in the lair of the Headmaster's wife and, although this was theoretically just another class, at the end of this year came the dreaded entrance examination to the local grammar school, with all the attendant pressures and hopes and fears which meant obtaining a scholarship or staying where you were. Although attendance at the grammar school was possible even if you failed to obtain a full scholarship, the parents had to pay; which for many meant that this was impossible.

This teacher did her best to force something in our heads which must have been a trial, and in some cases succeeded, but in mine was a complete failure and I only attained a half scholarship. We knew her as Polly because she had a deformed nail on her index finger in the shape of a beak and which she used to poke us with when she thought we were slacking. We wondered if we would end up with arms covered in indentations but this didn't happen and we appear to be fairly normal. We found her difficult to warm too and I remember her writing in my autograph book 'Don't try and lift yourself up by your bootlaces' which didn't have quite the same ring as Rob Gibb's effort of 'A rolling sausage gathers no gravy', the former being undoubtedly more worthy, but the latter more in keeping with a lad's outlook.

For those of us who, for one reason or another, didn't get the hoped for acceptance to the Grammar school, we now knew what it was like to be thought failures, for our last three years were merely filling in until it was time to go out to work. Our education, if it could be termed as such, was best described as fragmented, with male teachers seeming to come and go with some frequency. These teachers were men who were on their way to somewhere else, the first one being Mr. John Phillips, a tall Welshman who had been in post some time and was well thought of, being firm but fair. He also ran the village Boys Club so he was in our good books.

This teacher had a bell on his desk which he would bash the daylights out of when he wanted to obtain our attention. On one occasion needing to send one Freddie Kear for an interview with the head master, he had words with the lad as he got to the classroom door. He hastened his departure by throwing the bell at him, this being returned with interest catching Mr. Phillips on the knee, causing much hopping about and massage. One up to Freddie!

Then one morning the headmaster introduced a new teacher named Ossie White, who, according to the head was a Rugby player and would stand no nonsense. This man had a brief stay and was seen one day to have an altercation with one of our larger lads, which ended with the two involved rolling around on the floor of the classroom, with the headmaster hopping around the fringes in some alarm.

Then came a man who left me with little memories except the receiving of punishment for some misdemeanour or another. This was a Mr. Kennedy. Was it us lads who were at fault, or did the quality of teaching leave something to be desired. I wonder.

These men teachers were followed by a woman who introduced us to the classics and whose name escapes me but whose work I remember as being different and having interest for me, although it must be said that Shakespeare didn't go down well with us all. This was the best period of my school life and above all the introduction to poetry, which, with its rhythms and sounds gave me satisfaction and interest and which remains with me still.

She was what teaching was all about.

Mr. Sidney Miles, the headmaster had much else to do and left us to our own devices much of the time. Luckily he was keen on Maths and English and gave us plenty of both, although a lesson which was called "optional" appeared to be his favourite, in which one could read a book, or draw or do or do, more or less what one liked, as long as you were reasonable quiet. He also did his best to impress on us the virtues of honesty and good living, a favourite expression being 'I want you boys to be upright and down straight' backed by the application of the cane if he thought it necessary. If he caught anyone transgressing he could be severe, as happened one morning when my cousin spotted him on his way walking to school using his stick to help him down the rough track way, and remarked, "Here comes Sidney and his bloody stick".

Assembly that morning had the headmaster, complete with stick standing before us all and saying

"William, do you see something odd about this stick?"

And the reply

"No Mr. Miles."

Then again

"George, do you see anything odd about this stick?"

And again the reply

"No Mr. Miles."

And so on, until he came to my cousin and said

"Terence, do you see anything odd about this stick?"

And received the reply

"No Mr. Miles."

"But Terence," he persisted, "I distinctly remember you saying that this was a *bloody* stick."

Terence did not repeat the comment. He was a man of average height and build and seemed to favour grey suits, stiff collars and dark ties. He wore his hair with a quiff and sported a small moustache and was well thought of in our village, although to us he appeared an authoritative figure. He was also a very keen gardener and introduced us to working in the school garden, where we were taught the angle the spade had to be to put into the soil when digging, the ideal size for a seed potato (good hens egg) etc., which meant that the garden was the best in the village as pride was involved here. I never knew who had the produce of this blessed plot, but it went somewhere. Of course working in the garden was resented by some of us who took the view that there were other things of more interest than the best way to plant carrots or tie up runner beans, but I find it interesting to see how much of that gardening lore remains with me to this day.

There came a day however, when he announced that he had a load of manure to be moved from the roadside onto his garden, and that he would pay any boy who turned up with a spade a penny an hour to do the job. At that point we knew that Easter and Christmas had been rolled into one. He failed to realise that *any* boy in the school, irrespective of age or size who could carry a spade would turn up to earn his coppers, and it must have been a shock to his system to see dozens of boys of all ages descending upon that very large heap of manure and heaving it around like a horde of Chinese peasants.

To be fair however, he stuck to his bargain and paid up, and his maid spent a great deal of time running back and fore doling out lemonade to the mucky and smelly urchins who might have ponged a bit but were very happy. It was a great day. This could not be said for our mothers however when

31

we got home. I was stood outside the house and not allowed in before a good cleansing was administered.

So, while we were introduced to some aspects of education which we enjoyed, this was a very small drop in a very large ocean. We were more concerned with everything else that was happening at this time. During these last days before we were turfed out to dazzle the world with our industry, we were taught the skills it was felt that we would need, such as husbandry, how to dig the garden, how to make a dovetail joint, or use a chisel, or treat woolly aphis with a paint brush and paraffin on apple trees.

Not for us the esoteric subjects of the constitution or social responsibility or anything which might be deemed education and stretch our minds. I have thought in recent years if perhaps this might have been perpetuating a policy of keeping a body of labourers available and in their proper place.

So here we were, fourteen years of age, looking for work, some of us being lucky like myself and others drifting into anything that came up, such as the mines. Now the old associations started to break up with Reg going down the pit, Stan going back to the family farm, Owen becoming an apprentice electrician etc., sometimes not being renewed ever again. I am of the opinion that the greatest value of my education, if it could be termed as such, was being taught to read, because I then had the means to teach myself some of the things I was lacking. I was introduced to the world of books, and eventually completed my education. But, to a lad growing up in a village, life was exciting and full of incident as the war was raging and school was a back number.

Whatever any shortcomings that there might have been in our education, some things stick in the memory, such as sitting in the sun in the playground at lunchtime with ones back to the wall of the outside toilet block, munching on a sandwich, or kicking a tennis ball about the playground in a frenetic game of football of forty or so boys a side, and making slides in the Winter. There were also the time honoured games with conkers, marbles and the cards from cigarette packets, not forgetting the first puffs of Woodbine cigarettes, at two pence a packet of five cadged from the older boys. The problem with the smoking was that it was, of course, forbidden, and the lads had to go into the toilet for the surreptitious puff. Unfortunately, the urinal was open topped which meant that as the as the smoke ascended it could be seen from the teachers staff room, which meant that the headmaster would be waiting with his stick when the lads eventually appeared. Amazing that none of us worked out that the head wasn't clairvoyant!

Altogether our days at school were happy ones, as I remember, particularly the days when I went to my Grandmothers for lunch. In pre-war days it was possible to get bananas and the greengrocer nearby had his delivered in long orange painted boxes; which we imagined to be full of the black widow variety of spider and therefore deadly to our health and wellbeing. I never saw one of course, but I always stood well back after handing over my penny and watching him delve among the straw they were packed in to get me my solitary banana which I always had as part of my meal. He didn't seem to mind that it was just one and handed it over with a smile and a word or two; what a difference to the modern supermarket.

Jackie Jones was one of my best mates. He lived on the other side of the road from Grandmother, so that, long before I had finished my lunch, a head covered in a mass of tousled hair and completed with a grin which stretched from ear to ear would appear in the kitchen and say "has he gone to school yet?" well knowing I hadn't. The reason for this was that Jackie was aware that I sometimes had a penny to spend on sweets to munch on the way to school, and that I always insisted that if I had one, he had to have one too.

Having received our coppers from my indulgent Mother, we were out of the house in a flash, to sit on the garden wall and debate as to which sweet shop we were about to patronize.

Mrs. Knight, whose shop had rows of large bottles full of a galaxy of multi-coloured temptations which we were allowed to examine and discuss at length and decide whether gobstoppers or black striped boiled sweets were to be the choice of the day. Or the next one along who had packets of sherbet which was sucked up through a tube of liquorice and involved great industry and effort to ensure we had extracted the last possible atom of the sweet powder. Or Mrs. Blacks, who had an unsurpassed range of chewing gum which came complete with badges which identified the wearer as a pilot, a great soldier or some other hero. Or, in the summer, a call on Mrs. Woodhouse who sold home-made ice cream which we considered ambrosia and fit only for us and the angels.

I sometimes wonder where Jackie is now, and is he still taking so much time deciding whether to purchase gobstoppers or go all exotic with liquorice allsorts.

Chapter 4 A Boys Chapel

Our village was, many would agree, a throwback to Welsh revivalist times in relation to its religious life, although there were without doubt the usual selection of backsliders, rogues, fornicators and assorted villains as well as the sanctimonious, whiter than white, upright and generally good people found in any village in England, and us lads had a good working knowledge of many of both varieties.

The count of churches and chapels ran from the Church of England, whose vicar was an outgoing man not averse to the odd pint with the locals in a village pub, to the Primitive Methodist, the Wesleyan, the Baptist and even a Spiritualist chapel which was viewed by us lads, and many of the villagers with some suspicion, due to overheard comments of odd happenings at their meetings. There were also one or two chapels of indeterminate persuasion, so that the old Gloucestershire saying of "as sure as God's in Gloucester" because of the number of churches in the County was particularly apt when applied to our village.

My family were members of the Baptist church, which was perhaps the most popular in the village, but not rabidly Christian, forbidding anything which smelt of sin. Which was probably just as well as one or two members would have been on the brink of excommunication for sundry misdemeanors which were quietly overlooked. Indeed, it was rumoured that the Pastor, who was of a delicate disposition, was supplied with a glass of milk and raw egg laced with whiskey before entering the pulpit by a rather strait-laced lady parishioner. This I viewed with some doubt, but there was no doubting the fervour and fire of the man when he preached, and he certainly filled his church on Sundays and sent everyone home suitable chastised and terrified of Hell and damnation for the rest of the week, so that, even if true, he would, I am sure, have been forgiven.

He moved on eventually, no doubt sent to some other den of iniquity to bring the backsliders to heel, his place being taken by Arthur Price, a man who did much good for the village and his church.

One thing our chapel had over the other churches was the quality of its choir which was Miss Barrett's pride and joy. She was also the organist and I'm sure that that old instrument (the organ) nearly had a nervous breakdown every Saturday evening prior to her seating herself on Sunday at the keyboard. On special occasions such as festivals the choir came into its own, with suitable anthems and special items which deeply impressed us all.

My father had a decent tenor voice and was a member of this body, but I was particularly impressed by the family of Albert Jones. He had one of those deep bass voices which seem to come up from his boots, while his wife sang a lovely contralto and his daughter was good enough to have had training for her voice. I can still hear him putting in the descant in "Count your Blessings". It was worth going to church just to hear that.

One of my aunts was a very good soprano, and when she and Mrs. Jones got together to sing some of the old Welsh hymns it was a delight. I am sure that wherever these two ladies are now, and it must be heaven, they will be delighting the heavenly host with some of their offerings.

Mother, unfortunately, had no voice at all, but what she lost in tone she made up for in enthusiasm. When, on Sundays, she put on her hat and coat and made for her regular seat I'm sure the Lord warned his Angels and they all went for a picnic in another parish.

The bit of the Sunday service that we disliked most was the sermon, because it seemed to go on forever. We wanted to get out and away from grownups and, no doubt because we fidgeted and made noise, we were allowed to leave before the pastor got going. This gave us a chance in summer to walk along the railway line, there being no trains on a Sunday, and search through the ballast to find small stones which we used when playing five stones or jacks, or look for the small fruits of the wild strawberries which seemed to like growing on the railway embankments.

The one aspect of chapel life which affected us most was the Sunday school, which at our chapel was a large one of some 150 or so children. It also had a social side and, although it was one afternoon a weekend, we didn't really mind. It may also be the case that at the back of our minds there was the Sunday school outing which was a big day in our yearly calendar, and which could only be attended if you were a reasonably regular attendee at classes; and not turn up once or twice just before the event. As the time for the outing approached, excitement increased and much discussion took place as to its venue.

I am not sure why we worried about this, for we always went to the same place, a large playground at Bishops Cleeve, near Cheltenham. The man who owned the property was clever, in that he built slides of every description, swings etc., and put them under cover which meant that the weather was not a possible problem. There were also tables and benches to eat at, and for the adults to sit and gossip, so that everyone was catered for.

On the day of the outing, mothers would prepare sandwiches and fruit and include bottles of lemonade, and when all was complete would make their way to the chapel with their over excited families, where a number of buses would be waiting. Their drivers had that resigned look on their faces, usually found on those about to be hung or beheaded.

Having had roll calls made and lists checked, it was time to embark, and now us lads tried our best to get the back seat so that we could make faces at any following vehicles and generally be our exuberant selves; although the grownups sitting at the front kept us in some sort of order.

It was, of course, the case, that a trip of some 30 miles was the farthest that the most of us had ever been, and so there was plenty to interest us on the way, including the stops for those for whom it was all just too much and who were heartily sick.

On arrival the scene must have rivalled that of a disturbed ants nest as everyone rushed about looking to see what was on offer, and the noise made would have made a deaf man wince. Having been issued with a mat to sit on, to save our clothes when coming down the long slides, the day became a continuous climb to the top, a fast rush down and a climb up again, and, considering the number of lads and girls hurtling down at high speed and arriving at the bottom in a welter of arms and legs, it must have been a source of wonder that no breakages occurred, at least that I can recall. Maybe, as it was a Sunday school, there was some divine intervention! Whatever happened to anyone else on that day, to us it was a grand time, and we all went home thoroughly exhausted and sporting a bruise or two as trophies.

The other big occasion in our chapel calendar was the Sunday school Christmas Party.

This was always held in the large schoolroom, and with long tables laid out and groaning with delights such as cakes with icing, trifles, buns in profusion and nuts and fruit and other goodies, so this was a must to any lad. The teachers had gone to enormous trouble to decorate the room with steamers and paper chains and balloons, and with the two large stoves giving out a welcome heat we thought that we were nearly in Paradise.

The Chapel was on the floor of the valley and that evening saw lights moving down the footpaths through the Winter gloom and cold to this bright and welcoming place, and the arrival of children wrapped up against the cold but with shining faces and bright excited eyes, for this was just before Christmas and we were all living our dreams.

The noise inside the room was deafening, and I'm sure that the Superintendent of the school wished that he had a well-trained sheepdog available to herd the children into their allotted places, but I doubt if he could have found a sane hound to take us on, and that's just the girls.

However, at last we were seated at the tables, after having fought manfully to obtain the most favourable places within striking distance of the plates of sandwiches and cakes and other goodies.

Now, here we were, ready for the off, and then the call for silence for grace, during which, pairs of eyes were already weighing up the position of the cakes with the most icing and the sandwiches containing our favourite filling; although anything was very acceptable providing it wasn't fish paste.

But, although we were poised for action, there was one elderly lady who made even us look sluggards. She was a member of one of those families that every village has, whose members were avoided whenever possible, mainly because their version of bodily hygiene left much to be desired and were regularly acquainted with the cider bottle. She always turned up if a free meal was possible, together with a large bag, which she would proceed to fill, reaching across the table with the words "I'll have one of them, and one of them" until a helper removed what was left from temptation.

Needless to say we had our fill, and a good time was had by us all, the evening being complete when we were given a brown paper bag containing an apple or orange and a few nuts and were allowed to dip our hands in a barrel containing sawdust and feel around under the sawdust for a small present, to take home with us; the old faithful bran tub.

Of course, a Baptist chapel should have baptisms and ours was no exception.

To us boys the Sunday school and outing and attending the services when we couldn't get out of it was one thing, but becoming a fully-fledged member of the church was quite another. It meant that we were starting to grow up, and we were not ready for that.

However it was decreed that I, at least, had to be baptised, and so attended the classes which were supposed to explain what religion and the scriptures had to say about the way we should live our lives, and be as useful to humanity as possible. Just how much of this penetrated my head is open to debate, and I can't remember becoming imbued with religious fervour overnight; but I knew that I was going to be immersed in what I hoped would be water that was slightly warmed at least.

A baptism was, of course, a big day in the life of the church, and the building was usually full of regulars, and quite a few casuals who came to sample the excitement or just to see the candidates get well and truly wet.

Those youngsters who were the centre of attention had, of course, seen baptisms before, as the entire Sunday school always attended baptismal services; but now things were different and minds became focussed on the coming occasion.

The girls wore white dresses and the lads white shirts and gathered on the day in the vestry; the general feeling being of mild panic at the thought of being dipped completely underwater, particularly if you couldn't swim, and none of us could.

On entering the body of the Church we were met by the Minister, who rather resembled a frogman in a rubber suit without the flippers and the goggles. He instructed us what to do before our dip, which was to hold his right hand as he grasped us at chest level, whilst his left had us by the scruff of the neck, probably to prevent us doing a bunk. I think that if the front of the Ministers rubber suit had been painted white, he would have resembled a penguin hanging around an iceberg. Perhaps it was as well that no-one threw him a fish.

We were led in, one at a time, into the body of the church, to be met by the concentrated stare of a church full of people, some, no doubt, feeling glad it wasn't them stepping down into the waist deep water, and others, who were simply fascinated by it all.

After entering the water and listening to the whisper to keep the eyes closed and stay stiff, (which was rather misplaced as we were too terrified to relax anyway), we went under quickly and were on our way out almost before we knew what was happening. We then stumbled up the steps helped by a Mrs. Burgum who then threw a black cloth over our heads and led us back to the vestry and thence to the Sunday school building to dry off and get dressed into dry clothes.

As we emerged from the water the congregation sang the hymn 'Oh Happy day' which I never heard sung again for many years until a Gospel choir sang it during a radio programme, bringing the memories flooding back.

Although our experience of the teachings of the religious life didn't send us dashing off to a monastery or lead us to the Ministry, it didn't do us any harm either. At least that is my opinion, although some Atheists would argue the point I expect, and we felt that it was all part of village life, until life itself gave us much to think and wonder about.

It was after the evening service in summer time that sits happily on my memory, when my parents and their friends would stroll the half mile from the chapel to the banks of the river where village people gathered to exchange news and the current gossip. A small strip of the bank had been given to the people of the village by the Vaughan family of Courtfield for their use in perpetuity, and was known simply as "the Tump". A couple of horse chestnut trees gave shade and shelter if there was a scud of rain, and a few seats under them completed the scene. It was ideal for a little village bonding. Us lads larked about of course and occasionally stopped to look when a splash told us that a salmon had leapt out of the water trying to rid itself of the parasites under its scales. This was a magical time, when the air was warm, the swifts and swallows swept at the water level to take the flies and insects hatching on the surface of the river, the murmur of the water itself, the sight of the white flashes of the moorhens and their young, a few swans paddling about minding their own business, and the feeling that all was well with our world. If a God was anywhere, he was here, feeling very satisfied with himself.

Chapter 5 A Lads Families

My two families, Mothers and Fathers, were very different from each other. The Beard family originated, as far as I have been able to discover, in the area around the village of Saul, a few miles south of Gloucester, on the river Severn, and there is evidence of the name back as far as 1086 in Domesday Book. However, the need to find work and the social conditions of the time found them settled in the small town of Lydney, whence they gravitated to our village where they stayed and established themselves.

I hardly knew Grandfather Beard but he was a small man, and reputedly very strong. Certainly he was very virile as he sired twelve children, seven sons and five daughters, but before I got to know him well, he managed to fall some ten feet from a wall at his home, reportedly while pulling rhubarb, and broke his neck.

Grandmother was a lovely person whose father came from Wales to our valley to work in the production of tinplate. She always liked to give visitors a nice tea which, of course suited her grandchildren very well, and it was a great sorrow to her that she was unable to produce her usual cakes and other goodies as she became older, and infirm. She lived to the ripe old age of ninety two and was greatly missed when she died.

Of course with so many children, as might be expected, the older ones, especially my uncles, moved away from home as soon as possible, to find work and I suppose, make room for the younger siblings, so I didn't know them well.

All five daughters married local men and lived within four miles of each other, while two sons went into Wales, one to Birmingham, three stayed locally and one, a gifted engineer was sent to South Africa by the firm he worked for, took his family with him, and never returned.

As a group of people these uncles and aunts seemed to get on well together and all appeared to possess a dry sense of humour but came alive at Christmas time, when, as many families did, they all got together, if at all possible, at the family home for tea and an evening of family bonding.

This consisted of the men talking politics and generally catching up with news, while the women were more concerned with family and who, what and why were the family pregnancies if any, and if not, why not. And also who had done what to whom in the populace in general. We, the kids, were shunted into another room, to be not seen and not heard. This incarceration with other cousins whether we liked it or not, didn't endear me to them for some reason, but it was Christmas so we put up with it.

Of all the Beard family members my father was the odd one out in that he was the only one of his brothers to have any interest in sport of any kind. Consequently I was the only grandson to take part in any sporting activity. He was very good at any game he took up, particularly football and cricket, and I was encouraged to have a go at it all. He was a very handsome man and particularly fastidious in his dress. When preparing to go somewhere he would not be hurried by anyone or anything, but would continue to put on his hat at the right angle or adjust his tie to his entire satisfaction; even if the Devil himself was telling him to get a move on. This would cause the occasional difficulty when mother informed him that the transport conveying the team to a match was waiting and would he please hurry up. When the inevitable reply came, "If they want me they must wait", and because he was the captain and a good player, they usually did. Of course the time arrived when they decided that enough was enough, and they went without him, much to father's fury. He had a head of hair that was rarely ruffled and always immaculate whatever he was doing, and even when swimming always contrived to keep his hair dry, much to my amazement.

Whatever his foibles, he was a great father for a lad, giving time, help and encouragement when needed. As a little lad I would stand in the garden when he was due to come home from work and wait to see him pushing his bicycle up the hill. I would run to meet him, and be put up on the saddle, feet dangling and small arms reaching for the handlebars to be conveyed home in triumph.

He served in East Africa in World War 1 and contracted malaria which affected him in later years. However, he was a man who did not realise his true potential in life and his one regret was that, on his return from Service, he was offered the chance to join a transport company as a partner, as he could drive a vehicle, and turned it down; that company going on to become very large indeed.

Mother's family, the Wards, was very different and much more involved with village life. They, too, were a large family, of some seven boys and three daughters of which Mother was the eldest girl. This meant that, as the second girl went away into service with a local wealthy family and the youngest getting away with a good deal, Mother took the brunt of work in the family running her own home as well as her mothers. They don't come better than this.

Hilda was the second daughter and was in service all her working life, for the last thirty odd years working for the Royal family at Buckingham Palace; for which service she was made a member of the Victorian Order, the Queens own personal Order.

The Wards had a large house in the centre of the village with a shop attached and Grandma Ward sold china. On the weekend she baked a variety of delicious cakes for sale in time for tea on Sunday, which us lads had to deliver to the customers. Needless to say, we had our share of the goodies as wages, and I can almost taste the puff pastry and the jam and cream of those cakes.

While to us grandchildren she was kind and helpful when we needed it, she also had a rather sharp tongue which she applied to anyone in sight when it suited her, especially Grandad who would find interesting things to do on the garden when "she was in a talkative mood".

She also seemed very old to us as, like many older women of that generation, she wore almost exclusively black clothes, down to the ground, with hair dressed in a bun high on the head and with a small broach at the neck of her dress or a jet necklace when dressing up.

The family seemed to have a little more than many of the local people and I never knew where it came from; but one ancestor was a barge master working with river traffic on the Wye and the family had connections with a well-known wealthy Monmouth family.

Indeed, I never knew what Grandad did for a living. As an older man he used to walk about the village sticking up advertising posters on hoardings showing what was on at the cinema in the town nearby, what sales were on etc. I remember him having rolls of posters delivered to the house, and then he would pick up his pail of paste, collect a couple of children and off we would go, with us fighting to see who would carry the posters.

To us children he was gentle man, rather overweight and

sporting a large white moustache, and in a waistcoat pocket a small tin of hot, black sweets which we all doted upon. Whether it was the paste or the sweets he was our favourite.

Mother went to the family home most days to help her mother, which meant that, as a lad most of my time was spent there too. This didn't worry me much as there was a gang of us lads in the centre of the village. There was plenty to do from climbing a nearby abandoned quarry, to flying paper airplanes, to playing football on a bit of waste ground, and anything in between if it interested us.

There was a third member of my grandparents household, someone we called Uncle Fred, but who was my grandmother's brother, which made him our great uncle.

He always seemed ancient to us and was a real character, with his large moustache, a maroon corduroy waistcoat that he always wore, a shirt with no collar and an expression of benign amusement at the goings on of the rest of humanity. He was a cobbler by trade and worked in a large hut near his home. Because of this he was always known as "Sheddy Ward" but not to his face. That was always Mr. Ward, probably because he would take on the worst mending jobs, (men's pit boots and the like), and charge very little for doing so.

His hut had a large machine worked by a foot treadle which had a large number of disc attachments which polished, ground and did, (to us), all sorts of other amazing things. We would sometimes creep in and stand quietly and watch him work, smell the new leather and gape as he shaped a new sole with his razor shape knife. Our being there didn't seem to bother him, and that hut was a place where we spent many happy hours.

He was, perhaps, the slowest man I ever met in his actions. He walked slowly, ate slowly and did everything at a snail's pace, until it came to hammering nails into a new sole for a shoe, and then he was like lightning in his hand movements. Many times I watched him having a boiled egg for his tea, and wondered whether the egg on the spoon would ever reach his mouth, but it got there somehow, probably cold, and it didn't seem to bother Uncle Fred.

He was a fascination to us lads, but he was quiet and tolerant with all the grandchildren and we liked him. I think there was more to our uncle than we appreciated, because being a bachelor and a very quiet man, he perhaps felt more than he said or showed and this was exemplified by the following story.

My Grandmother's kitchen was large and had a partition around which all us kids would swing when we ran in. On one occasion, at a sad time when a cousin named Mary died of some illness, my mother told me that Uncle Fred swore that he saw Mary run into the kitchen and swing round the partition, and they found out later that this was at the very moment that poor Mary died. I don't know the truth of it but perhaps our well-being and lives were felt much more deeply by him than we knew.

My uncles were a lively lot and very close knit as a group, and I think that my mother had more influence over them than their real mother had, as they all seemed to come to her when they wanted advice or were in trouble.

Uncle Jim was the youngest uncle and had the unenviable reputation of being the man that no-one wanted to stand by when watching the local football team play. This was because he was a passionate man by nature, and right was right, and if the referee didn't see that the opposition was well offside just before scoring the goal he was going to tell him so, and anyone else who happened to be within 100 yards.

To see Uncle Jim starting to get steam up on a Saturday afternoon before the match, even before the start, he would be convinced somebody was cheating, was like watching Vesuvius grumbling away just before the eruption which destroyed Pompeii. But, to be fair, everyone on the football pitch came within his sphere of insult, friend and foe alike, and after the match, win or lose, the team selectors were routinely consigned to Hades as certifiable lunatics, knowing nothing of the players or the game in general.

He had played the game in his youth and was known as a half-back, who took no prisoners and gave no quarter and asked none, but this was in the days of knee length shorts, stiff leather boots and a leather ball, and anything sticking above the grass was to be given a good kicking.

He was a good uncle to me however, whatever his faults. As he and his wife were unable to have children, they gave me many treats, such as a trip to Gloucester on the bus at Christmas time always with a half crown in my pocket to spend on some toy or other, (a cowboy hat or a submarine which when wound up and put in a pond actually went under water and the reappeared again when the spring had wound down), followed by a nice tea every Sunday. I was glad that they eventually adopted a son who became a credit to them.

Another uncle was Henry, always known as Harry of course. He was much quieter and reserved, but with a well-developed sense of humour. He lived close to grandmother's house and so we would come into contact quite frequently, which was very pleasant as he was a kindly man who would help where he could and was always even tempered with us lads.

Now, it should be known that the one thing us lads lusted after was a bicycle, which was the last thing we or our parents could afford in those times. It didn't matter what sort of machine, or how old, as long as it had two wheels and moved.

Then, on a never to be forgotten day, I was sent on some errand or another to Uncle Harry's and, on being told where to find him, which was a lean-to building attached to his house, found him pottering about at his workbench.

The thing which caught my eye, however, was a bicycle hanging on two nails hammered into the wall. It was an old bicycle, dusty with scabs of rust on wheels and handlebars, but, as far as I was concerned it was made of solid gold.

I couldn't take my eyes off that old bike, which must have become obvious to my uncle for he said "would you like that bike my boy", to which I of course replied "Yes please". Could he mean it, did he mean it?

"Well," he said, "you can have it, but you must buy it, and it will cost you two shillings and sixpence".

I have to admit that my first thought was horror. Where could I find that amount of money as it seemed an astronomical sum? Then came disappointment that my uncle was going to charge me for an old bike when he wasn't using it, and didn't want it.

But I agreed to pay that amount, and went away to start saving every penny I could from any source possible. Gradually the pennies and the very occasional three penny piece mounted up until I had it at last, the cost of the bike.

So, off to see Uncle Harry, who had taken the bike down

from the wall where it had hung, and cleaned it and made it rideable. To me it took first place to the chariot which took Elijah to heaven. Uncle took my money, and then, to my astonishment handed it back saying, "There you are my boy, and there is a lesson for you. Always save for the things you want and don't borrow to get it. Now go and buy a tool kit and bell for your bike, and don't fall off." Dear Uncle Harry. Loved and hated at the same time, but never forgotten.

Of the seven of my uncles, only two moved away to work; one in Yorkshire and one in Wales. Both did very well and prospered. They were very close knit as a family and if one was in trouble there was always someone at his back.

This was illustrated at the beginning of World War 1 when all the lads, as one, including their father, walked three miles to the local railway station to catch a train to Monmouth to enlist, and grandfather was only persuaded to go home when the womenfolk found out what had happened and sorted it all out before irrevocable decisions had been made. Two of those same uncles were awarded medals for gallantry which says it all for my uncles.

Chapter 6 Escapades and Odd Balls

Although the war years changed our childhood irrevocably, the life for us lads prior to this was, in many ways idyllic.

The pace of village life was slow, we felt safe and secure, although we were unaware of the sacrifices being made by our parents to keep us in that condition. We knew, more or less, what we could do and where we could go and keep out of trouble, and we had thousands of acres of hillsides and woodland to run wild over. The result was a feeling of freedom within the restriction of our village morality and unwritten rules.

It would, of course, be unreasonable to expect a bunch of lads to be as white as the driven snow all the time, and I am quite sure that if they were here now they would agree that there were times when we were more like a section of the junior mafia in our silence over some exploit. For instance there was the matter of the shed.

This was made of corrugated iron, painted black and belonged to a local man of rather uncertain temperament. If we were passing along the lane which ran along the side of his garden, and he happened to be digging his potatoes or some other job and he spotted us, he would shout and tell us to clear off whether innocent or guilty, or he would have the law on us.

It would be fair to say that he had some reason for his animosity, because in retaliation it was not unknown for us to throw a half brick against his shed, which made a satisfying crash and was guaranteed to bring him out after us; particularly if he was inside it, and then take to our heels.

On one occasion, however, the elderly man was waiting for

us, and, as the first stone hit the shed he leapt out of his garden gate giving a fair impression of a tiger with his eye on a gazelle that was not quite quick enough. In this case the target was a cousin who was also not quick enough, and who was hauled off by the scuff of his neck, amid threats of summary justice being administered.

We were now in some dismay as we needed to get Terrence back, preferably in reasonable order, but the thought of confronting our irate gentleman was daunting to say the least.

After some thirty minutes or so and no reappearance of Terrence we were thinking of invoking Habeas Corpus, when, around the corner appeared a lad, one Kenneth S, who was a couple of years older than us and of a more sober character, and whom we descended upon. We persuaded him, against his better judgment he said, to approach our adversary and ask for Terrence back.

He, without doubt had great powers of persuasion, because eventually a tearful lad appeared together with threats of what would happen if we threw any more stones. This kept us quiet for some time and well away from the shed, and very quiet about the whole thing, for we would have been in trouble if anyone had talked. Unfortunately for the old gentleman, another group of lads did the same thing the following week. The old black shed was certainly battle scarred.

There was, of course, always something which our parents would rather that we did not do, and in some cases there would be a complete ban imposed. In my case this was swimming in the river.

Other than the fact that I couldn't swim at all at the ripe old age of seven, which was a consideration, the river Wye is a very dangerous river to take chances with, claiming one life per annum even now, when this sport seems to hold no attraction for lads of today. This is because the bed of the river is very uneven, with rocks and holes and therefore not suitable for wading, while the coldness of the water can bring on cramp and the currents can drag one under very quickly.

But, for all this, there was always some intrepid lad who was prepared to risk life and limb for the sake of a dip, and one favourite spot was at a place called the Black Bridge, mainly because it *was* black and spanned the river, carrying the railway line.

On this occasion I had gone out with some of the lads, and eventually mother noted that I had not returned for some long time and, on enquiring of an older lad if he had seen me about, received the reply that I had gone to the Black Bridge with a bunch of lads who were going swimming.

At this point, mother's mind went into free fall, and she saw me floating downstream never to return. She therefore took off, still in her wrap-around pinafore, some two miles to where we were, on foot, at great speed, like some avenging Fury, to find me sitting happily on the bank watching the rest of the lads.

Whether it was anger at me for not telling her where I was going, or relief that I was all right, she was rather upset to say the least, and on the way home with her hand on the scruff of my neck, it was impressed on me that it must never happen again. When aroused, mother could be very forceful, and it didn't happen again. She also impressed the dangers on the rest of the lads, although, as one pointed out, there wasn't a swimming pool within a six mile radius, so what else could they do?

Another time honoured pastime we indulged in round about harvest time was that of scrumping for apples, which, of course was illegal, but which didn't deter our band of junior villains. If a local orchard had a particularly good crop of russets or some other favourite variety, it was not unknown for lads to take a sample, illicitly, to try.

Usually the local owners didn't seem to mind too much, as very few used or stored all the fruit they grew, but were satisfied with chasing off the culprits, and I cannot remember a time when Sgt. Ireland of the Police was involved.

One such owner was an elderly widow called Mrs. Meredith, a lady who was always dressed in unrelieved black and wore large hats of the style of the First World War. She was a thin person, and although well into her seventies, was extremely fast on her feet. Getting away with a handful of her delicious plums was a challenge which I think we both relished, and certainly she never complained to mother, although I'm sure she knew who we were.

There was one orchard, however, which posed a real challenge. After one occasion, when one evening about dusk one of the gang was sent through the hedge to see if there were any apples he could shake down easily, the owner suddenly appeared carrying a lantern. The lad up the tree froze with terror, and was further concerned when the owner put down his lantern and sat under the tree. After some fifteen minutes the lad up the tree was in a state of panic, when the owner said "Well my boy, I know you are up there and you had better come down." The lad obviously thought this was a case of death or glory, dropped out of the tree and made a run for it, only to get stuck in the hedge, head first, which gave the owner a very decent aiming point, which he took full advantage of. It was one up to the owner.

Although swimming or scrumping apples were risky in some ways, there were other things we did which could have caused real damage to life and limb such as racing on made up bicycles.

This involved finding a bicycle frame that had been thrown away, hopefully with a pair of handlebars and front forks. Old wheels with no tyres were fixed on with bits of metal and there were no brakes, pedals or saddle. A rolled up sack was tied on to make something to sit on. These lethal contraptions were then taken up a wooded hill and ridden down again at high speed, with the only way to stop being to fall off.

What with trees, gullies, banks and other assorted dangers it was only providence which prevented mass slaughter. Of course our parents had no idea what we were up to, which was just as well. The odd thing was that, in fact, no one did get killed; but there must have been many near misses.

Another escapade involved the carbide which the local miners put in their lamps to give light when underground at work. Many of the men used to carry the lamps, which were quite small, on the front of their caps, held on with string, and would take off the lamp before getting home and knock out the spent carbide on a convenient stone. There was one stone which the miners seemed particularly attracted to, and so, sometimes, we would find carbide which had some life left in it. This was scraped up and then put in a bottle and corked, having been watered in the time honoured method.

The idea was to put the bottle in a hole in a bank, put a piece of paper or some such in the neck to light, and wait for the ensuing explosion, which I never remember happening. If, in many years' time an archaeologist turns up a lot of bottles in holes in banks with a paste of carbide in them, and wonders what it is, he can send for us and we will enlighten him! We certainly wouldn't have made good explosive experts, that was sure, but we must have enjoyed the expectation of causing raised eyebrows among the adults if it had come off. We didn't think of the potential damage to ourselves, of course.

There were, of course, in our village, as in every other village in England various characters whom we took for granted, but who would today be looked upon as definitely odd. As, for instance, the man who would take his horse and dray some six miles to pick up a large quantity of live elvers (baby eels) in a zinc bath, and then sell them to housewives in the village.

These elvers were grey in colour, about two inches in length, said to be very nutritious, and were considered to be a delicacy. I remember my grandmother buying a pan full and frying them in a batter so that they were crispy to eat. They were also considered to be a very effective aphrodisiac, as grandma, who had ten children would perhaps testify. This seller of elvers had a habit of stopping at each public house he came to, so that, by the time he reached the last one he was singing hymns, and his rather large nose had attained a very rosy glow. The pub customers would then lay him on his dray, have a word with his horse, who would then take him sedately home, elverless but happy. It is virtually impossible now to buy elvers as they are now exported to Japan etc. and cost a fortune to buy. There are no sellers of elvers like him left either.

Another was the local pig sticker, as we called him. It was the case that, in those days, many local people kept a pig on their property which supplemented their food supply, and which, at the appropriate time was killed and made into bacon and other delicacies. There was nothing wasted from those pigs, and it was common for a family to kill their pig and share some of it with neighbours. I wonder if that would happen today. There was no local abattoir where the pig might be killed, and regulations didn't exist for this activity, and so, enter the pig sticker.

This man was middle aged and lived with his widowed mother on the edge of the wood. He seemed to shave but rarely, and when he set out to kill a pig he favoured an old fashioned suit, a cloth cap, a neck scarf and carried his knives in a roll of cloth in his pocket, and was altogether like someone from a Dickens novel. Whatever he looked like, he was of interest to us lads and when he was seen setting out on business we might be seen not too far away. Of course the pig could be heard squealing all over the valley, prior to his attendance, but we were a blood-thirsty lot and wanted to be in on whatever was going on. If the truth were told I don't think any of us were too keen on the business. It was probably the fascination of it, and I don't think any of us ever spoke a word to the pig sticker.

There was one lady who lived in our part of the village and whom we knew as Aunty Fanny, although she wasn't really an aunt. But to us she was just Aunt Fanny, and that was the way it was. She was, as they say, well covered, and well into her sixties and was the possessor of a voice which could take the skin off a rice pudding.

Now it so happened that I had had an altercation with my mother, and had decided to leave home, never to return, which was some decision for a little lad. Off I went in high dudgeon, no doubt with my steps becoming slower as I realised the action I as pursuing. After about four hundred yards I met Aunt Fanny who was sitting outside her house, and who, in the manner of village neighbours, wanted to know where I was off to.

I explained the situation, and was invited into her house for a piece of her cake, as she suggested I needed something to eat before starting out. Of course, after a little while I was walking back home, holding the hand of Aunt Fanny. I found out later that my mother had watched me all the way. A very nice family were the Whittington's.

Another lady who was of interest was Miss C. She was someone of indeterminate age but must have been in her sixties. Wearing an old coat, a knitted bonnet, and skirts which always seemed to be six inches too short, so that her harvest festivals (all is safely gathered in) were all too obvious, and stout boots. She would appear at grandmother's door, usually toward the end of the day, tap on it, and come in.

A common occurrence in a village you might think, but what was uncommon was that she had with her two pails of milk. This milk she sold as she went through the village, and grandmother would have a pint or two, although our milk was normally delivered by a local farmer by horse and trap, the housewife taking out her jug and having it filled from a churn.

Miss C lived with her two brothers on an isolated smallholding some two miles from the village, on the other side of a wooded ridge. She had carried her milk all the way and must have had the strength and stamina of an Olympic athlete. After chatting for half an hour or so she would be up and away to her next port of call and then walk home in the dark.

Would they do that today, even if they dared? I think she was simply a very lonely person, and just wanted to make sure that there were other people in the world. She was probably glad too for the few coppers she made from the sale of her milk.

There were, of course, other characters in the village, from those whom every one avoided if possible, to the ones who were not averse to carrying home a salmon or a meal of salmon fry if they jumped up and fell in their pocket. Or those to whom a chicken or perhaps somebody's prize cabbages were an irresistible temptation. We knew most of these people, and they didn't bother us lads, they were just part of the life around us. Where are these characters now one might ask?

The acquisition of the odd copper was always in our minds, and weddings were always good for replenishing our depleted stocks. The idea was that the gate to the bride's house was tied so that she couldn't get out until we untied it, which required reward, and also that the route to the church would see lads with raised ropes across the road refusing to let the bridegroom's car pass until a few coppers were thrown out of the window. This was known as roping a wedding and woe betide the best man who forgot to have a pocket full of coppers.

But funerals were also to be looked at, and we would sit and watch the cortège pass, being carried by his friends, with the men in front and the mourners behind the coffin, the men wearing black bowler hats and best suits. Everybody walked at a funeral, even the mourners and the men in front would halt at the lynch gate, part (they walked in pairs), let the mourners through and then follow behind into the church. What a difference today. We were very solemn watching a funeral.

Although any pennies we managed to accumulate were spent on sweets and suchlike they also became useful on a Saturday night at about six pm when the local cinema opened for the first house showing of whatever was the going films. The cinema was, in fact, the local Memorial

Hall, built to commemorate those local men who had been killed in the First World War, being also used for dances and all sorts of local goings on.

It was quite large as this kind of hall goes, and for the cinema had chairs for the adults and several rows of wooden forms at the front for the children. It also had a balcony with tip up plush seats, the ones at the very back being doubles, thus giving ample room for couples to indulge in a heated bonding session. Many a couple could be seen to dash out, rosy cheeked and with a silly smile on their faces before the lights came up.

It being a Saturday, it was the day when Grandma and Mother were elbow deep in flour and the ingredients of the delicious cakes which they made for sale to the villagers for tea on Sunday. It was a good business for the cakes were good and sold well; being hand delivered by us grandchildren after chapel.

I was therefore sent off to the cinema, out of the way, with a couple of mates, with five pennies in my pocket, four for a seat on the wooden forms at the front and one for a large packet of peanuts (monkey nuts to us) to chew during the performance, bought from the shop of Mr. Gibbs who was also one of the village bakers; a good friend of mine, as one of my uncles had married one of his daughters.

Now the man who ran the cinema was our old friend Mr. Sidney Miles our headmaster, as you will remember. His wife sat in a cubicle and took our coppers, while a young man called Williams, who was a mechanic at the local garage, worked the projectors and took the brunt of the groans when they broke down, or the film failed for one reason or another. This was very public spirited of them both, particularly as poor old Mr. Miles suffered apoplexy every time we all turned up.

This was because the monkey nuts we had bought were in their shells and these shells were discarded at our feet, which, when a lad or girl wanted to go to the toilet were trampled underfoot, making a noise much akin to the annual migration of a herd of wildebeest through a patch of dried grass. This racket went on for several minutes, and all that could be heard was the adults as one man hissing "quiet, and sit down".

This would bring Mr. Miles dashing down the aisle as he tried to ferret out the miscreants but he rarely had any luck, and as the whole thing happened again five minutes later anyway, he was in great danger of saying hello to St Peter before his time.

So us lads sat and suffered during the big film and all the soppy stuff waiting for the cowboys and Indians to appear. Tom Mix and Gene Autry were our heroes and we knew that when they turned up all would be well. Then it was over and off we went giving our mounts the whip and spur until we got home and until we could ride the Wild West again next Saturday.

Back to Grandmas kitchen and the cake baking. Sitting in the warmth and watching Great Uncle Fred's herrings being toasted in front of the fire. A little bit of heaven for a very drowsy lad.

Chapter 7 A Boys War

Of course, the run-up to WW2 was, for us, fairly meaningless in that although we heard of places like Czechoslovakia, Poland and Austria having trouble with the Germans, they were far-away places inhabited with people who were definitely not English and therefore to be viewed with the utmost suspicion, and anyway we had lots going on in our lives.

The day that war was declared by Mr. Chamberlain was rather odd, as my father joined our neighbour and several others, gathered around a radio set. Everything seemed rather solemn although the sun was shining. I heard the announcement and remember the sound of his voice, and he sounded to me a tired, sad man, something I remember still. The men listening said little and soon went home and, at that time, I felt something had changed, but didn't know what it was.

As time went on we heard and read of the progress of the war, but this was the first year, and the only thing we noticed was a number of young men from the village who went missing for a time and then reappeared in uniform looking extremely smart with a shine on their boots that put the sun to shame. They looked proud and ready for anything and we were somewhat envious of them.

These men were, of course, reservists, and as we had only seen policemen in uniform, they were something of a novelty. But then we noticed our fathers and older men getting together in a basement room of the local memorial hall, (built as a remembrance of that earlier conflict), and then wearing armlets with the letters LDV, which, of course, meant Local Defence Volunteers but which soon became Look, Duck and Vanish.

This, of course, was unfair as these men wanted to do something and the call had gone out for volunteers to be there to take a part if the enemy appeared. This was a possibility at that time, and they would have made a difference as there were many veterans from WW1 in villages and towns who had had combat experience and could still load and aim a rifle; even if failing eyesight meant that in some cases they were probably a greater menace to their own side than the Germans. Of course, that early in the war there were no rifles or other arms to be had, and a few shotguns were not going to cause much bother to a few Waffen SS Grenadiers. But, no doubt, they remembered the words of Mr. Churchill, 'they also serve who only stand and wait', and did what they could. But things distinctly changed when Mr. Philips, one of our teachers, was seen in a Special Constables uniform, (as if he didn't already give us enough trouble), and even mother donned the dark blue dress of an air raid warden. Father became a Lieutenant in the Home Guard as it became known as, complete with WW1 medals and sporting a swagger cane.

Things became much more serious when we heard the news that Ralph, who was someone we knew, and the son of Mrs. Woodhouse who made our homemade ice-cream, had disappeared at the evacuation of Dunkirk, never to be heard of again. The poor lady could not get over his loss and for the rest of her life believed that he would be back sometime, and was probably a prisoner of war somewhere. His death cast a gloom over the village, as he was the first one of the village to die, but unfortunately it was not the last.

Now, had we but known it, the childhood we knew had gone, never to return. In the entire village there were no more than twenty street lights, in whose beams we played, or just hung around as lads do, of an early evening, and these had now gone, and darkness seemed blacker for it. Also, it was a time for the issue of gas masks, to be carried round in small boxes, and I recently came across two photographs of all us schoolchildren standing in the playground wearing our gasmasks. And of changes in the things we ate, as some food was rationed such as meat and butter and eggs, and bananas and oranges were unobtainable. I sometimes wonder how much sacrifice was made by parents of their rations so that we could have as much as possible.

No longer were we playing at Cowboys and Indians on the hillsides and in the woods, banging away with toy guns and a strip of caps and falling down very theatrically stone dead, or fighting with sticks instead of swords and never being hurt. It was now a matter of, can I get into a uniform, (not to fight at this time, of course, but because we wanted to be part of the excitement). It didn't matter what colour, or service, as long as we could be seen in it by the girls at the school and any friends who hadn't one.

Of course this was a forlorn hope, and the nearest any of us got to a promise of action was as a messenger taking information to and from the headquarters, (there were no field telephones or radios of course), which we had to accept; the junior cadet forces not being available to a twelve year old for a couple of years.

But there was always something to attract our attention, such as the sight of a neighbour, festooned in bracken so that he looked like a walking haystack, trying to hide on a hillside. We had been doing this all our young lives and he wouldn't have stood a chance!

The time then came when firearms became available for father and his mates, together with Denham uniforms, and then regulation army issue uniforms. This was of interest, as

Sunday mornings became firing practice day, and the village reverberated with the sound of gunfire from a local quarry. We were not sure if they hit the targets they had set up, but they certainly frightened the local crows to death, and did little for the peace of mind of the horses.

It wasn't long before uniforms of other units, other than the Home Guard appeared. They were members of the Pioneer Corps, and were mainly foreign troops from countries such as Poland or Czechoslovakia, and who, in some cases had brought their families with them. This, of course, caused local problems as to where accommodation could be found, an example of this occurring when, one evening at about 8pm there was a knock at the door, and on answering it I was confronted by two dark shapes. On closer examination they turned into a soldier and a small woman who was carrying a baby wrapped in a shawl.

I called mother who entered into a long conversation with the two people, the upshot being that the woman and child lived with us until the soldier was moved on. I overheard mother telling my father that there was no way that she could turn away someone with a child in arms at that time of night even if she was saving a bedroom for our London relatives if they were bombed out and needed refuge. They were a decent couple, and we all got on well together, whatever the strains, as tended to happen in those times, when a little give and take was the order of the day.

We should have remembered this when these troops formed a football team to play our village team, many of whom on taking the field proceeded to pull women's hairnets over their rather long hair. This, to us lads, was good for a laugh and comments that this was going to be an easy victory against a load of girls was rife. The only excuse for these ungracious comments I can make, is that the accepted thinking of a lad in those days was that England was England and therefore right and proper, and anything foreign was definitely below the salt. But, whatever we thought, the reality was that the visitors gave our lads a lesson in how to play football, hairnets notwithstanding, and we went home rather chastened.

The job that these men did, was to erect thousands of hemispherical, open ended shelters made of corrugated iron some 12 feet long and 6 feet or so high on the sides of roads, under the trees, and in many places making new ash roads through the denser parts of the woods for more shelters.

This seemed odd to us lads, but all was revealed when American troops arrived to fill them with shells and other munitions, so that the area became a huge ammunition dump. There didn't appear to be any guards to keep us out, but needless to say we kept well away from the contents of the shelters, and at the start of the invasion of Europe they suddenly emptied in what seemed to be a very short time.

Whereas the Pioneer Corps were of all sorts of nationalities and got along together, the Americans were strictly segregated by the colour of their skin, black in one area and white in another, although of the same army and nation. With all these varieties of troops and refugees about the area there were the usual problems of brawls over girls or drink, and of some local girls being no better than they should be, but being lads of 14 or so we managed to keep out of trouble even if they didn't.

It would be fair to say that, in general, our war disrupted our education and lives and changed the way we looked at life. It also altered the route our future lives were going to take, but in comparison with other lads in other cities and towns we had little to grumble about. And particularly when watching the red glow in the night sky as Bristol burned, or seeing other lads in varying states of trauma brought to our village for respite and healing from London. Though perhaps we didn't understand fully what it all meant, we knew things were not as they should be, but didn't know what to do about it.

As the war years passed we realised that we might be involved and so some of us started to get interested in the various Cadet Corps, such as the Air Training or Army Cadet Corps. This took up two or three evenings a week in a nearby town and, as I had always been interested in flying, it was air training for me.

So, together with a few other lads it was practicing Morse Code, learning about principles of flight, and navigation by star charts, together with foot drill etc. twice a week and then parade on Sunday morning in the playground of the local Grammar school. We were very proud to be strutting around in our uniforms and, as we were now beginning to take an interest in people of the female persuasion, our shoes were polished to a mirror shine as were buttons and anything else which might attract.

Of course, we were also able to take trips in service aircraft now and then to whet our appetites, usually in training aircraft which circled over the Severn estuary dropping dummy bombs, or some other forgettable activity. Though we gained nothing by all this, the one thing I learned was that I was severely airsick as soon as I put one foot aboard. As it didn't dawn on me to take stomach calming tablets, even if there were such things in those days, I still went along for the ride. However, I certainly didn't enjoy the experience much, particularly as we were informed very firmly that if you were sick in the aircraft you would have to clear it up. Suitable bags to be sick in were a must with most of us.

As time went by and the war continued, it was time to give some thought to the service in which one would serve. On reading of the exploits of the aircrews of the Fleet Air Arm in the sinking of the German battleship Tirpitz, and the destruction of the Italian fleet at Taranto, I decided this was for me. And, anyway, I thought the uniform much smarter, although the idea of landing an aircraft on the pitching deck of an aircraft carrier did cause one to pause for thought.

At the age of sixteen I volunteered and was accepted under what was known as the "Y" scheme, whereby one would be trained as aircrew. This was something I was very pleased about as I could now wear a white flash in my cap, but the deflation came when I was told that I would be sent for when eighteen, and, in the meantime must do nothing to bring the service into disrepute.

But all this is another story.

But, before leaving the war and how it affected us lads, I would mention the following.

It was about this time that we were beginning to attend the local hop, or dance to you, and to be suitably equipped I borrowed my father's patent leather dress shoes, unknown to him. So, off I went with a couple of friends in a bid to cut a dash and break the hearts of as many females as possible. The evening was successful and after the last waltz we three could be seen escorting two young ladies home through the blackout.

We had to pass a small telephone exchange on our journey which was being guarded by the troops of the Home Guard and, on approaching the spot a voice boomed out of the darkness "Halt who goes there", to which we correctly replied "friend". Then again the voice" advance friend and be recognised". Now with some trepidation we walked forward into the light of a torch to be examined by the troops, after which, with some relief we were told to "pass friend", which we did rather swiftly before there was a change of mind. But, when we were nearly out of earshot I heard my fathers' voice say. "I'll talk to you about my shoes in the morning and don't be too late". Needless to say I was the cause of great merriment, and my romantic promise suffered a severe setback. Thank goodness it was dark and, as the scripture says, be sure your sins will find you out.

So the war for us lads was a time of change, with a very great deal going on. So much, in fact, that boredom was never a problem, and it was a matter of packing everything in. But we managed it somehow, and though we lost our more peaceful lives and we don't know what these would have brought, I doubt if any of us regret this upheaval to our restricted village lives and our exposure to times we could not have dreamed of.

Chapter 8 A Lads Occasions

To a young lad there was always something going on in our village, but sometimes there were special occasions, such as bonfire nights, Christmas, and when it snowed.

The preparations for bonfire night and the celebration of a traitors demise might be considered macabre to some, particularly being burnt to death in effigy, but I'm sure that we didn't see it that way, and most of us didn't know the full story anyway.

These preparations took at least three weeks or more, as a bonfire had to be built, guys made and paraded round the village in the hope of attracting the odd copper and, if our funds ran to it, the contemplation of what fireworks we were going to let off.

So now it was making guys time, with every small gang finding old trousers, coats, hats and boots, and dressing up bags of straw. Then it was putting them into an old pram or box on two wheels and wheeling them around the village with the cry of "penny for the guy, penny for the guy, put him on the bonfire and there let him die" in the hope of meeting someone with money and the urge to distribute it.

There being little money about, we had few coppers to spare, so there was much consideration given on the relative merits of penny bangers, squibs, jumping jacks and packets of sparklers. Sometimes an indulgent parent would provide a rocket or two, but the main event was the bonfire.

The decision to have a bonfire being made, a suitable piece of waste ground was selected and fuel began to be collected. The news soon spread, and soon lads and girls, in fact anyone who could carry a stick or something which would burn, appeared, dumped their load and returned for more. The whole thing resembled an ant's nest, with the ants working at top speed.

Usually the fire was constructed by an older person, such as a father or older brother with tendencies toward arson, to prevent serious danger to life and limb of us lads. I believe that they secretly enjoyed themselves. Then, at the appointed hour, just as it was getting dark, we all forgathered, children and parents, and the people who had built it, succumbed to the urge to set fire to something. We would then stand gaping like a bunch of Neanderthals at their first sight of fire, until it was no more, and all the fireworks had banged and fizzed and shot up into space. And then home in the dark, promising to build a bigger one another day.

November the eleventh, Armistice Day, was an occasion which always impressed this lad. Those who had lost husbands, sons, or men of their families, gathered together in the village hall and it was a time of solemn thoughts, reflection, and shed and unshed tears, so that the hall was filled with their heartache. Men wore their best suits, and with the medals they had won shining on their chests, marched together behind the banners of the British Legion to pay homage to those missing from their ranks. The women, of course came too, and others to support them in their grieving.

I have visited that village hall recently, and stood in front of the brass plaque bearing the names of the fallen, picturing again the flowers surrounding it, usually chrysanthemums it seemed to me, smelling them. I have thought since those days, that, as the flags dipped, the bugle sang it's sad call of the Last Post, and the words "They shall grow not old..." were spoken, did some of the men assembled there see other things and other places.

Did Uncle Bill see the broken bodies he brought in from the mud of Flanders?

Did Uncle Harold see the drab brown rocks and desert as he held off the attacks of the Turk?

Did Uncle Alf see the barbed wire and huts of the prison camp in Germany, and did my father feel the heat of Africa, facing the diseases of black water fever and malaria?

I wonder. They never spoke of it.

A very solemn occasion and one I didn't know I would repeat in a later time and with more names on the plaque. Will we never learn?

An occasion which always stirred the spirits of us lads was the first snowfall of the winter. Then there could be heard much sawing and hammering, as odd bits of wood were fashioned into a vague resemblance to a toboggan, (known as a sledge to us). Not for us the shop bought variety, as we hadn't the money to buy one, and it was more fun to make one of our own anyway.

If we had been employed in the building of Noah's Ark, it would have been built in half the time, but would have most certainly sunk, as our efforts at carpentry left much to be desired. But, nevertheless, we persevered, and eventually dragged our efforts out to the slopes, of which there were plenty in our valley. From the nearly flat to the suicidal, all had their share of takers.

One in particular was long and very fast. At its lower end a small-holder had built a lean-to to house his goats. When a lad travelling at near supersonic speeds hit it broadside on the goats, no doubt considering discretion to be the better

73

part of valor shot out and disappeared toward the horizon at a very high rate of knots. I don't remember the aftermath of this, but I'm sure that the goats never forgot it, and it certainly livened up their day.

As well as sledging, there were the usual slides made in the school playground, the making of snowmen and the snowball battles. The fact that we all got very wet bothered us little, as we were overheated by our exertions. Whatever grown-ups thought of winter snow we didn't know or care. To us it was a source of excitement and fun, and always looked forward too.

Christmas was, perhaps, the biggest occasion in our calendar, when everything seemed to be happening. Not that there were parties every night, not in our village, except the one at the Sunday school described earlier. But we were off school and it might snow, if it had not done so already, and there was a general feeling of excitement and expectation, a time when something was different.

We hadn't the money for buying presents, although we might have had a copper or two earned through carol singing; but with our voices, that could never be guaranteed. We did hope, however, that our long suffering parents could find something to make our day.

Any presents we received were usually in the singular, such as a Meccano set, or something to make or build, but we always hung up a stocking more in hope than anger, and somehow it always had some small thing inside, such as a sugar mouse or a trinket or nuts and an orange when the morning came. In this we were very fortunate, as in those days there were many others who had little or nothing.

Prior to the event we went through the ritual of sending

messages to Father Christmas up the chimney, in the hope that something might get through, but goodness knows what the birds thought of it all.

The school helped to work us up to a froth by getting us to make paper decorations by sticking strips of paper together with glue to make paper chains, which was a very hazardous occupation for a gang of ham-fisted delinquents like us. But we enjoyed ourselves no doubt, and the classrooms looked very pretty.

In the early years there was always the Nativity play, when chequered tea towels and sheets came to the fore, and parents and grandparents turned up for the laughs. Now was a time when embryo actors and actresses could be found in every corner of the school, and harassed teachers contemplated taking a long holiday in Brazil or some other far flung hideaway.

On one, never to be forgotten, occasion, someone decided in their wisdom, to put on a school concert. Of course everyone had to have a part to play, if only singing in the chorus. Unfortunately, I was one of those given the black spot, and had to be on stage in full view of my admiring parents and other poor grown-ups. The other participant in this extravaganza was one June H who, while being a perfectly nice girl, was just not my cup of tea. Not only that, we had to sing, and the ditty went thus:

June sang, "O soldier, soldier, won't you marry me, with your trumpet, fife, and drum?"

To which I replied, "O no sweet maid I can't marry thee, as I have no gloves to put on."

The chorus then chimed in with, "Then off she went to her

grandfather's chest, and brought him a pair of the very, very best, and the soldier put them on."

And so on with shoes.

This all seemed quite innocuous, but something went wrong with the synchronisation of the singing and the putting on of the gloves/shoes etc., so the thing ended with me, very red-faced but struggling manfully to put gloves on hands that had too many fingers, and shoes that appeared to be two sizes too small, whilst the audience was in hysterics. Not my finest hour, and it was many years before I trod the boards again. Fame was not for me, but still, it was Christmas.

At Christmas time it was the custom in our family to go to one of our grandparents for lunch and the other for tea. While in both cases family members turned up, it was the lunchtimes best remembered. A few days beforehand grandfather was sent out to get a couple of chickens for the table. Not for us the turkey; this was unheard of in our village, and as the birds were our own, costs were kept down.

At around ten o'clock in the morning, mother would be sent to the cellar with a large enameled jug, to be filled with elderberry wine with which to toast the King after his speech, this being placed on the hob to mull. Unfortunately, grandfather's chair was also close to the fire, and, as the temperature of the wine had to be monitored regularly, the jug ended up slightly depleted, and grandfather's face carried a beatific smile and a very rosy hue. A lovely man. Then, after lunch, off to the other grandparents for tea, and more relations, and bonding. Now all is changed, as it must be, but for this lad, Christmas was a wonderful time, never to be forgotten.

Well, that's a few musings of those times that must have been for us halcyon days, had we but known it.

May all your days be halcyon days.

Collected Verse

The Actor

I'm thinking of taking up acting again
Yes, treading the boards, as they say.
Once more to be king of theatre
I can't wait to get in a play.
I've been approached by a Director,
Who said that he wanted the best
And please could I be there next Monday
To give the old tonsils a test.

Of course it has never been easy.
A critic said I made him sick
And that they should pay me to just stop at home
And please could I show him the trick.
But, as Gielgud said of my acting,
That he'd always be in my debt.
That he'd never seen anything like it
And would certainly never forget.

It was when I was playing in Hamlet.
And was scaling the highest of heights,
The cheers could be heard from three streets away
When I tore a large split in my tights.
But I was determined to finish the scene,
An actor is used to distractions
Then somebody yelled though my acting was poor
He could certainly see my attractions

The audience one night was quite silent,
So I knew there was reason to hope
That tonight I was going to get my reward
When a voice said "I'm getting a rope."
Then, as I attempted to finish the scene,
The people arose as one man
Demanding my head be stuck on a pole,
The rest of the cast simply ran

The Police took me down to the station,
Inciting a riot they said,
The Magistrate said I should serve thirty days
And thank goodness no-one was dead.
So, up until now I've been resting
But soon I'll be back on the stage,
So do come along and see me perform,
You see, I'm the best of the age.

A Chocolate Treat

I'm sitting in this fancy box
Just waiting for the day
When someone says 'a chocolate whirl,
I'll have that if I may'.

I'm very grand as chocolates go,
the best choc known to man,
my place of birth was Belgium,
now beat that if you can.

My friends are very special too
atop the chocolate tree,
there's champagne truffles, strawberry creams
yes, most select are we.

We're very social chocolates
but can't stand common toffee,
nor do we like the nutty ones
or those containing coffee.

But most of all, the ones we hate
are hard ones wrapped in papers,
they really get us most upset,
and gives us all the vapours.

So here reclining in our box
we make a splendid sight,
and if you'd like a sample
then why not take a bite.

A Warning

What can we say of this, our life
If all it is, is stress and strife.

And we neglect those we should cherish,
Close mind and heart, before they perish.

And not a contact, not a thought,
A card to write, a flower bought

How sad it is our lives are driven,
And not a smile or word is given.

For we will find one sad, sad day
That all those friends are gone away.

And suddenly our breast is bare
Of those, our friends, who used to care.

The saddest thing for one to hear?
When someone says, maybe next year.

Saturday Sports

I'm fed up with sport on a Saturday
And taking you two to your game,
Yes, I know you're selected to play in the team
But my life's no longer the same.
I've had quite enough of this chauffeuring lark
And I'm thinking of going on strike,
if you don't start getting a move on at once,
You'll just have to go on your bike.

Yes William, I know that it's rugby today
And I said I'd take you and your mate,
That the kick-off's at two and it's now half past one
But there's no need to get in that state.
You'll find your boots just where you left them my boy
Which is probably under your bed,
And here are the socks that you gave me to wash
Yes that's right, ones green and ones red.

They were not the same colour when you brought
them home,
And they'll look rather odd I agree
I don't know what you've done with the others,
I just wash 'em so don't look at me.
The shirt you brought home was a perfect disgrace,
You must have been rolling in mud,
And though I know rugby can sometimes be rough,
This stain on the sleeve looks like blood.

I'm not waiting all day for you Brenda,
Find your kit and then get on and pack,
And just be more careful with that hockey stick
I just saw you give William a whack.
I know he's a nuisance and gets on your nerves,
But to cripple him just isn't fair
And don't you dare give him another,
Just because he was pulling your hair.

And I'm sure it's not true that you hate him
So kindly let go of his coat
And William, she'll not get to hockey today,
Or at all with your hands round her throat.
I do wish you two would stop fighting,
And be pleasant and nice for a change
But if you prefer to live ten miles apart
Then I'll see just what I can arrange.

Now come on you two, have you packed all your kit,
William, why are you making that noise,
It's a bit late for mending a split in your shorts,
Does it matter you're playing with boys.
And Brenda come here and stop sulking,
There's just nothing wrong with the skirt,
You're going to be playing a hockey match girl,
So a crease isn't going to hurt.

That's it kids you've just got two minutes
To get yourselves out of the door,
Or I'm off to get in some shopping
And I'll never take you any more.
Brenda, stop waving that stick in the car
Or I'm sure you'll be doing some damage,
No William you're not going back for a wee,
We're just off so you'll just have to manage.

Here we go, at last, roll on Sunday.

Music

The Thrush sat in the treetop,
Singing his heart out for joy
As he poured out notes of liquid gold
On a still and listening world.

What a racket, said the crow to his mate
As they listened nearby, I'm off,
And away they flew, cawing happily together,
In harmony, one taking the melody
And the other the descant.

Which goes to show that it takes all sorts
To make music.

The Young Piper

For Francesca, my young piper.

Oh, play me a tune young piper,
Come, play a fine tune for me,
Of misty moors, red heather clad,
Where grouse call out to greet the morn
And stag and hind roam, wild and free.

Of lochs, whose beauty fills my heart,
A song of streams and braes,
Of mountains, where few feet have trod,
Where eagles soar and ride the wind,
A tune to last me all my days.

Or yet, perhaps, a lilting tune,
A tune that calls to one and all
And bids them come, their feet to tap
Their hands to clasp, their eyes to shine,
And join their partners at the ball.

A jig to dance, to leap and swing
Or yet a strathspey, danced with grace
And then, perhaps, a merry reel.
The pipers tune will lead the way
To laughing lips and happy face.

Now play for me a marching tune
That leads the feet o'er hill and dale.
A tune that lightens heavy loads,
And makes the journey shorter seem
If feet should falter, spirits fail.

And now a tune that's wild and fierce,
A tune that sends men out to die,
That has been heard the whole world o'er,
A tune we should not wish to play,
And men who hear it might ask why.

Now, one last tune I beg you play
Young piper, of your charity,
When I can no more hear your pipes,
And you should think me worthy
Then play a sad lament for me.

Neighbours

My neighbour will keep borrowing
My tea, my bread and jam,
And now she's started popping round
To borrow soup and ham.

Last Sunday she sent round her lad
To see if I could spare
A cup or two of sugar
White or brown, she didn't care

Then could I let her have a pinch
Of coffee, just a jar
As long as it's Columbian,
As it was best by far.

She then asked for tomatoes,
Only one or two she begs
And have you any mushrooms
To go with ham and eggs.

I'll let you have it back she says,
Tomorrow never fear,
But she's still got my pasta
That she borrowed back last year.

I do begin to wonder, just
What will she borrow next,
And if I haven't what she wants
She tends to get quite vexed.

Last week it was the mower,
Could I spare it for a day,
And have you any petrol
I could borrow, if I may.

But now I'm really worried
For two days ago she came
To borrow Joe, my husband
To mend her window frame.

I don't know what he's doing
But he hasn't reappeared,
But as she never gives things back
I think it's as I feared.

But I don't really mind at all
For now the thought occurs,
I rather fancy Fred next door,
I'll go and borrow hers.

Have you noticed

Have you noticed
That as you get older
You become of less relevance
To younger people than you.
It's as though you are
Gradually becoming invisible.
It starts at about the age of 10.

Have you noticed
That by the age of 15
Little bits of you have
Started to disappear,
Just around the edges.
It's something to do
With make up and boys.

Have you noticed,
That when you are 25 lots
Of you have disappeared..
It's something to do
With micro skirts, way out
Pop groups and that you
Have left home.

Have you noticed,
That when you are 35 whole
Chunks of you have disappeared.
It's something to do with
Clothes, and music, kids and
Clubbing.

Have you noticed,
That when you are 45
Arms and legs have disappeared.
It's something to do with
Not playing rough sports
Joining the WI and being
An expert on real ales.

Have you noticed,
That when you are 55
You are definitely dimmer.
It's something to do with
Being a grandparent, joining
The National Trust, wearing
Designer glasses and the Soaps.

Have you noticed
That when you are 65
You can hardly be seen at all.
It's something to do with
 Bus passes, pensions, wearing
A lot of crimplene, beige, and
Having a shampoo and set
Every week.

Have you noticed,
That when you are 75
You have only a toe or two visible.
It's something to do with
Hair and teeth and the
Ability to only make love
Only twice a night.

Have you noticed,
That when you are 85 you
Have disappeared altogether
To everybody, except 10 year olds.
Have you noticed ------------.

The Fairy on the Christmas Tree

I'm the fairy on the Christmas tree,
I'm in my Sunday best,
They've tied me to the highest branch
With wire around my chest.
But still I feel I can't complain,
 At least I can be seen
Not like that Father Christmas,
But we know where he's been.

He comes down through the chimney
Bringing down a lot of soot,
And leaves such mucky footprints
Everywhere he puts his foot.
It's really quite annoying
As round the house he scurries,
To leave his presents for the kids
And then away he hurries.

It's just as well that humans
Can never see the mess,
And as for all those reindeer,
They're no problem I confess.
But I can't help but worry
As he sometimes gets quite merry,
That one day he'll be breathalysed
When he's been drinking sherry.

Some people think they'd like to be
The Fairy on the Christmas tree,
And I admit it's lots of fun
To laugh at all the things you see.
But when they stick you up on high
Beneath a light that flickers,
They never think you're standing with
Pine needles up your knickers.

But I don't mind there's always things
To make me feel quite jolly,
To see the baubles on my tree,
The tinsel and the holly.
It made me smile when Granddads' pipe
Set fire to Grandmas' hat,
And Roger used the tree lights
To electrocute the cat.

And when last year the relatives
Turned up all bright and perky
To sample lunch and poor old Dad
Forgot to cook the turkey
Then, when she joined in blind mans buff
Amid the festive capers,
Aunt Ethel grabbed a sausage,
And gave herself the vapours.

I know I shouldn't laugh of course
It really isn't fair
When things go wrong at Christmas time
And me without a care.
So have a lovely Christmas time
And every time you see
A Fairy smiling down at you
It might be little me.

The Wise Owl

When from my nest I flew last night
To try and find a decent meal,
A mouse perhaps, or any other
That scuttles or runs and has appeal.
A sudden thought occurred to me,
Which wasn't really a surprise
Because we owls are said to be
Thoughtful and clever and terribly wise.

That thought is one I often have,
Whenever I go out of nights
When skies are clear and looking up
I see a host of twinkling lights.
I wonder what they really are,
And is it true, as I have heard
That they are holes to let through rain,
But that, I think is quite absurd.

Others, it seems, are quite convinced
There's someone they call God and Lord
Who sits up there and watches all,
But if that's so He won't get bored.
Because there's really quite a lot
Of birds and beasts and fish and things
That crawl and climb and live in holes
Some with tails and some with wings.

So, how can He see every one
And, if he does, how can He care,
He'd have enough to do, I think
Just holding on, to stay up there.
No! I'm really not convinced as yet,
That someone who's omnipotent
Lets humans act the way they do,
And yet create the firmament.

I think I'd rather give my trust
To our Great Owl, so wise and good
Who tells us we must do our best
To live our lives as wise owls should.
Doing no harm to man or beast,
Look after others who can't fly,
And even if we don't succeed
To do all this, well we should try.

So, as I sit upon my stump
As evening falls, and hear the cries
And songs of all my feathered friends,
I often just philosophize
On where us birds and beasts fit in
With humans and their awful ways,
Because they just don't care at all
If this great world they might erase.

I wish sometimes they'd go away,
And leave the rest of us in peace,
Then we could get on with our lives
And all the nastiness would cease.
Then I could see the sky at night
And know without a single doubt
That all those myriad lights up there
Would stay alight and not go out.

What's in a name

It started the day I was christened
When the family were there in their droves,
There were Grannys and Grandads and cousins galore,
And me in me christening clothes.

Even Great Auntie Gwen who was ninety turned up
With her perfume of camphor and gin,
And Uncle Bert who'd had a whisky or two
Asked if we could please carry him in.

The verger said he'd never seen such a rush
As we all converged at the door
But gamely he managed to wedge us all in
But the kids had to sit on the floor.

The vicar was quite overcome by the crowd
But manfully fought through the mob,
Using elbows and feet to get up to the font
So that he could get on with the job

He set off at once at a gallop,
But something just didn't seem right
When he started the marriage service instead.
Then we knew that the old boy was tight.

The organist said he was often like this
But was sure everything would be fine,
That he'd given some very fine sermon
After drinking communion wine.

The Churchwarden said that he'd prop him up,
And to stop now would be such a shame,
And so they started again and it all went quite well,
Until they arrived at the name.

What's the name of this child he enquired of my mum,
But before the poor soul could be heard,
The family all shouted the name that they liked,
So the whole thing became quite absurd.

Oh dear, said the Vicar now what shall I do,
While the verger just fainted away,
The Churchwarden said why not give him the lot,
So he did and that ended the day.

Oh! I do wish I knew what my name is,
Or rather which one should I chose,
You see I have dozens to choose from, And I really
don't know which to use.

I think I'll make it Fred.

The Typist's Dream

I wish I belonged to a girls band
With me eyelids all coloured bright blue,
And me earholes all battered by crotchets,
Though what they are I havn't a clue.
I'd have me three mates in the setup
There'd be Blodwen, I know she'd be keen,
She has a nice voice and could stand at the back
And rattle her big tambourine

Then there would be Madge who'd be great on guitar
And although she seems rather quiet
When she waggles her hips and it all starts to shake
The front row will undoubtedly riot
And lastly there's Vera, a ravishing blonde,
Who'd be plucking away on the base,
We could easily cover her pimples
By sequins we'd stick on her face.

I'd be the lead on the vocals,
With a routine to drive men insane,
By winding me legs round the microphone stand,
And saying yeah now and again.
I'd have a red blouse which was split to the waist
And me hair I'd have coloured bright green,
With a short micro skirt I'm quite certain to be
The swingingest chick ever seen.

Of course we'd have a nice name for the band,
Like the Beatles, the Stones and the Might,
I've decided to call us the Budgies
Cos we're pretty and ready for flight.
We'd need an arranger to fix up the songs
And we'd have to be sure he's in place,
'Cos Blodwen is purely falsetto,
Whilst Vera can only sing base.

A couple of dressers for make -up
And sort out our costumes and hair,
A driver to make sure the minibus works
As we travel around here and there.
A chap who'd look after the fan club
And an agent to book up the hall,
A technical bloke who would switch on the lights
And a tour manager and all.

So, farewell typewriter I'm off with the girls
And farewell to old Ross-on-Wye,
For we'll be taking show business by storm,
We'll show 'em that we'll do or die.
And it's hello to London, the grand Albert Hall,
The Budgies you're stage will adorn.
The music worlds' waiting to welcome us girls,
Yes, four superstars have been born.

The mighty Road Cone

I'm sure you must have seen them.
There's millions I've been told,
They seem to stretch for miles and miles
Just standing on the road.

We humans call them road cones,
In number they just thrive,
And though they never seem to move
Those road cones are alive.

It's true, I saw one smiling
As it moved an inch or two,
Then standing quite immovable,
Refused to let me through.

Their numbers are increasing
Exponentially it seems,
They appear to be encouraged
To fornicate in teams.

Where do I get my proof you say,
These things are procreating,
Well, I have witnesses who say
That they have seen them mating.

It's on the backs of lorries
That it happens, so they say,
Before they jump down on the road,
To start their happy day.

Reports have said it's possible,
That there's a central brain
Directing where they travel to
To block up every lane.

Some people think them aliens,
From somewhere out in space,
And we're completely brainwashed
By this mighty road cone race.

The Government should start a cull,
To bring their numbers down,
Before they try to infiltrate
The streets in every town.

I think it really is their fault
This problem they've created,
So they must start to put it right
Before we're inundated.

It may require the Army,
The Marines or S A S,
To trim their numbers back a bit,
And help clean up this mess.

And what can I do, you may ask,
To stem this great invasion,
Just knock them over I suggest
Whenever there's occasion

This might just get them worried,
As they stand there night and day,
And if you do it often
They might even go away.

So, start the fight back straight away,
Go out and kick a few
nd show them that we're willing
And our English hearts are true.

We're not afraid of road cones,
We'll neither yield nor bend
Our knee to any road cone,
We'll fight right to the end.

A Ladies Lament

Why don't they make stronger elastic,
The stuff which will never give way,
A good solid product us ladies can trust,
Giving confidence throughout the day.
For there's nothing that's quite so alarming
When standing in front of a group,
As feeling a snap and a slither
And knowing you're right in the soup.

You stand there immobile, your brain gone to sleep
You go pale and you feel your heart sinking,
For you're sure that the ladies are all on your side
But you know what the men are all thinking.
It just isn't fair that it's always the girls,
And the thought which to me really rankles,
Is that you but rarely see men blushing pink
Looking daft with their pants round their ankles.

Just think of the Queen standing stately and grand,
When she knows with a heart beating quicker
That she'd be expected to take the salute
Whilst clutching a handful of knicker.
So come on designers, just give us a break
And listen to this maidens cry
Make the frothiest, frilliest ones that you can
With elastic on which we'll rely.

Armistice Day

The Flags dipped
The bugles sounded
The people stilled.
Thoughts crowding in.
They never found Ralph after Dunkirk,
Or Kenneth, lost in the jungles of Burma.

Two men in an army of ghosts.
An army who had few doubts,
Who believed in what they were doing
And left recriminations to others
Who couldn't understand
They gave willingly.

Not their lives, of course
For no man does that,
Except for your child
Or a great love.
But they risked their lives willingly,
And for that we give them honour

But, how many stand with bowed head,
Empty, except for wondering what's for lunch.
Or whether United will win this afternoon
And isn't two minutes a long time.
But should we be surprised
For we know none of these ghosts.

For grief is often a private thing
Not to be paraded by the nation
As some sort of virtue they have to indulge in.
But then, perhaps they recognised
That someone was saddened and perhaps
They also felt a little guilt.

For should we not also give honour
To the policeman shot by the lawbreaker
Or the fireman, buried under a burning roof
While trying to rescue a family.
And how many more risk their lives
That others may live.

So, when once again the flags dip.
The bugles sound.
Let us be still
And let our thoughts be with all those,
Quick or dead
Who willingly risk all for us.

For they, and we are all part of the whole.
Even although to many
Gratitude is misplaced
And they pass by unthinking.

First love

Mary Dewhurst fell in love one shiny summers morn
A love she felt she was destined for
From the second she was born.
She stood transfixed when she saw it,
One shaking hand to her breast,
Her mind a mad turmoil of passion and lust,
Her heart almost burst from her chest.

It stood there alone on the forecourt
'Neath a banner which said, take me do
I'm not too expensive, just two hundred pounds,
Take a look, I've been waiting for you.
It's colour was a midnight blue,
It's lines were both bold and yet sleek,
It seemed to say I'm the finest small car
That you'll find any day of the week.

With murmured endearments and quickening breath
She ran her hand over the bonnet,
And when she caught sight of the gear stick,
She could nearly have written a sonnet.
The salesman said that he hated to part
With such a remarkable car,
That you'd never see anything like it again,
Just the top of the models by far.

But Mary just knew that this gem must be hers
Though the engine wouldn't start,
And then when a mirror came of in her hand
It nearly broke her heart.
"It's obvious you've been neglected," she cried,
"But I'll soon put you right never fear,"
But, just then the gearbox fell out on the road,
Which caused her to shed a small tear.

"I don't care, I'll still take you," said Mary,
As she struggled to open the door,
Then found she was viewing with horror
A rather large hole in the floor.
"How dare they," she wept "it's outrageous,
To let you get into this state,
But I'll get you fixed in a jiffy
And running before it's too late."

But then came the realisation,
Which cut like a knife through the heart,
She'd only got sixty three pence in her purse,
Which wouldn't have bought a spare part.
"Oh, what shall I do," said poor Mary,
"It's getting you right is what matters,
And all that I have is a handful of pence,
All my hopes and my dreams are in tatters"

There, there," said the salesman, a handsome young
man
As he patted her tear stained cheek,
"You can take this fine vehicle home with you now
If you pay me a shilling a week."
"Oh you darling," said Mary "then that's what I'll do,"
And she gave him a great big kiss,
"Well I'm jiggered," the salesman said "that's very
nice,"
"You can call round here anytime miss."

So Mary went off with the love of her life,
And, armed with a paint pot and polish
She set about bringing her love back to life,
The rusty old parts to abolish.
Though everyone said it was loves labour lost
She knew her first instinct was right
As she tenderly polished his chrome plated bits
While she worked through the dead of the night.

At last came the day for which she had longed,
When her true love again saw the light,
It sent Mary into a lather
At such a magnificent sight.
She knew then it would always be her first great love,
That they'd be together for life
That they'd never be known as two singles again
They would always be just car and wife.

I shouldn't have gone to that Doctor

I shouldn't have gone to that Doctor,
I'm quite sure that the man is a quack
He says that he thinks it's my gallstones
But I know that it's really my back.

He looked in my mouth and said "Blimey,
Your tongue is the strangest I've seen,
It's not so much that it's twelve inches long
But I've never seen one that's bright green.

Of what it was causing the problem
He certainly seemed rather vague,
But it wasn't the measles and could be the croup
And, if not, then it could be the plague.

By now I was feeling quite restive
As he asked me to take of my vest,
But then he suggested I stand on one leg,
And had I been feeling depressed.

At this point the called in two colleagues
Requesting their help and advice,
One took a good look and then fainted,
The other was off in a trice.

"I should check your heart and blood pressure" he said
"Though there doesn't seem much point,
Your colour keeps changing from blue to bright red,
Which seems to suggest it's a joint."

"Now, something I think I should mention,
You do have a very nice cough,
And that toe looks as though it has gangrene,
But don't fret we'll soon have it off."

I said "tell me Doctor, if you'd be so kind,
Do you think there's cause to worry,"
"Well, if you're thinking of buying a suit, he replied
I think that you should hurry".

He then said "I'll test your reflexes,
To check if there's life there at all,
I'm not at all sure you're living,
Is there someone you'd like me to call".

I shouldn't have gone to that Doctor
I'm quite sure that the man is a quack,
He said "come and see me a fortnight from now"
But I really don't think I'll go back.

Ode to a Haggis

They strode along the moorland track
In rough inclement weather,
But rain and wind could never spoil
Their walk among the heather.
The Scotsman blithely led the way
The Englishman behind,
The land was empty, not a trace
Of any humankind.

Then suddenly the Englishman,
In tones both loud and shrill,
Cried "Stop, and tell me what is that
That moves on yonder hill".
The Scotsman stared a long, long time
Then said "I must conclude
It's just a wee bit Haggis
That is foraging for food."

"But they're extinct" replied his friend,
"You're incorrect I fear",
"The last was shot near Blair Athol
Whilst savaging a deer."
"Preposterous," the Scotsman said,
"Although it's rather dark,
Did you not see it had six legs,
And did you hear it's bark."

"You're right," the Englishman replied,
His face alive with rapture,
"Just think how famous we would be,
If that Haggis we could capture.
And then, when we had trained it
We could put it on a lead
And walk it right down Princes St,
That would be fame indeed."

The Scotsman said "I'd rather not
For I have heard it said
When cornered they're ferocious,
And you can end up dead."
"Well, I shall catch that haggis
If it takes me half a year,"
Proclaimed his friend, "and I'll
Subdue it never fear."

So through the snow and wind and rain,
That haggis did he track,
For twenty years he hunted it
From South to North and back.
One year he nearly caught it when
The creature stood at bay,
But as he reached to grab it,
That haggis slipped away.

And then at last that Englishman
Was never heard of more,
His search became a legend, and
The stuff of Scottish lore.
And it is said two ghosts are seen
In some far moorland place,
A haggis, and an Englishman
Continuing the chase.

The last of the Christmas Puddings

I'm the last of the Great Christmas Puddings.
The last of a vanishing race
The last of that succulent, glorious band
To look a roast spud in the face.

Mind you, it has taken some doing
To keep myself out of the flow,
And when they grabbed Albert, my very best mate
I must admit that was a blow.

Of course there are thousands of puddings
Still waiting for someone to buy,
But for the superior puddings like us
I assure you, we don't have to try.

You see, we're not made, we're created,
Our ingredients none but the best,
In fact it was said that the vicar was asked
To ensure that us puddings were blessed.

The family all joined in the stirring of course
Made a wish, and then took a turn,
But when Grandma said that she'd lost her false teeth
Well, it certainly caused some concern.

But, at last there comes that finest hour,
That we puddings have yearned for all year,
When ladies all quiver in anticipation
And even strong men shed a tear.

Yes, it's Christmas, and family and friends all turn up
And crowd round the table for lunch,
And though there is turkey and lots of nice things,
We know we're the best of the bunch.

Then at last comes that magical moment
With everyone nearly replete,
When somebody cries "where's the pudding,
I'm still waiting here for my treat."

And time just stands still at that cry from the heart,
And we puddings just quiver with pride,
For we know that they're waiting to set us on fire
And there's custard with cream on the side.

But please, don't feel sad at our parting,
Indeed there is cause for elation,
For puddings like us are immortal and so
Just be there at our next incarnation.

And next time you sample a glass of old port
As you sit by the fire, feeling mellow,
Just remember the last of the puddings, and
Raise a glass to that famous old fellow.

The Ballad of Billy

Young Billy is a little thug,
He's getting like his dad

And though it seems he's getting worse,
He wasn't always bad.

When he was six he ran the streets
But had the biggest grin,

A face that shone with innocence
With not a sign of sin.

He hadn't much in worldly goods,
His boots showed signs of wear

His food was mainly bread and jam,
But Billy didn't care.

He didn't know he was deprived
Although his teacher worried,

Of many things he might have had
As home to mum he hurried.

Because he knew, when he got home
His mum would smile and say,

And here comes Billy my big boy,
What did you do today.

She'd hold him close and kiss him,
The world a place apart,

But Billy couldn't see the pain
Within his mothers heart,

For she knew, as all mothers know
That time would strip away

The childhood trust and innocence
Just a little day by day.

Until at last her Billy
Would end up worldly wise,

The kind of man we'd made him
No matter how she tries

To hold at bay the tides of life
In which we all must sink,

To keep him clean not tainted
By a world that doesn't think

Of what it does to children,
What it takes and not return

All the laughs and tears and sorrows
And the lessons they must learn.

How would it be if, once a year
Mankind could once more find

That innocence and trust we had
But now have left behind..

The Blackthorn Hedge

It is a tall hedge, twice my height.
A twisted mass of black branches.
A threatening hedge, daring anything
To try and push through it.
With thorns. A nasty hedge.
All Winter I have passed that hedge,
Hunching my shoulders
Against it's blackness and threat.
I felt shrivelled up at the sight of it.

But I know, that one day,
When the sun has warmed that cold hedge
In the Spring before the leaves appear,
That blackthorn hedge will be covered
In snow white tiny blossoms.
Then I know my heart will lift,
I shall take a deep breath
And feel as though I am swelling with joy.
That life is returning and the Earth has
Turned once more.

Every year that hedge reminds me that
Change is possible, that the blackness
Can become white,
That despair can become hope,
That life returns and continues.

The Challenge
Or, The Saga of the Marrow

Dai Jenkins loved his garden,
It was his pride and joy,
He planted carrots, Brussels sprouts
Potatoes and savoy.
Lettuce and purple sprouting
Courgettes and runner bean,
They really were the finest veg
That folk had ever seen.

But Megan, Dai's devoted wife
Grew tired of staying home,
Whilst Dai worked his allotment
And she was left alone.
Thus came a time, remembered still
By Welshmen to this day,
"I'll beat him at this gardening lark"
A neighbour heard her say.

"I'll suggest a competition
To decide which of us two
Can grow the biggest marrow,
He'll see what I can do."
When Dai came home he laughed aloud
"Right love" he said "we'll see,
Although I'm very certain
That the winner will be me".

Now, news of Megan's challenge
Was reported far and wide,
And the females of the nation
Were all on Megan's side,
And, as Dai had the men's' support
Debate was soon quite heated,
And language used by either side
Just couldn't be repeated.

So, seeds were planted, rules were made
To ensure there was fair play
And teams of volunteers were set
On guard both night and day
For sabotage was talked about
As leaves broke through the soil,
For betting was quite frenzied
And was coming to the boil.

Dai used the very best manure
His growing plant to nourish,
And gleaned advice where're he could
To make his marrow flourish.
Whilst Megan simply talked to hers,
In whispers soft and low,
She'd heard it was the thing to do
To help make small things grow.

And so those marrows grew apace
With speculation rife,
As which of them was now in front
Dai Jenkins, or his wife.
Trips were arranged by charabanc
As crowds of people came
To share in the excitement,
Such was the marrows fame.

And then, at last, came Judgement day
A day when time stood still,
When every Welshman held his breath
And birds forgot to trill.
The Welsh Assembly was convened
And, after much persuasion,
It's Leader came to be the judge
It was a grand occasion

And so they gathered solemnly
Around the mighty pair,
Anybody of importance came
Just dying to be there.
Dai thought his marrow just in front
And now, to make quite sure
He gave his plant a final boost,
A bucket of manure

The marrow couldn't take the strain
In this struggle to be first,
It gave a whimper, then a grunt
And then that marrow burst.
 Then Dai knew he was beaten
He was a broken man
While Megan felt superior,
As only women can.

And what became of Dai you ask,
Is he alive or dead,
Well, Dai went into exile
Into England, so it's said.
Whilst Megan had her marrow stuffed
Then later put on view,
And women flocked to see and stare,
And so her legend grew.

And so the challenge ended
Megan's honour satisfied,
But something didn't seen quite right,
For she felt cold inside.
No smile was there for comfort
No arms to hold her tight,
Instead a large stuffed marrow
To cuddle to at night.

What is the moral of this sad, sad tale ?
It is this.
If you are out in front along life's journey,
Don't throw a bucket of manure over yourself.
Or you might go pop.

The Screwmaker

I am a trained screw makers mate,
I make screws by the million,
I'm trying for the record
To make 'em by the billion.
I press down on this handle
And then I press this knob,
Some people think it's boring
But I just love the job.

I'm trying for promotion
And they say I'm right on track
To win the yellow Tee shirt
Which says Gaffer on the back.
But, if the boss can't see my worth
And this ambition fails,
I'll transfer all my expertise
To making six inch nails.

A husbands lament

I'm sure that my wife is clairvoyant
As she seems to sense my every move,
And though she denies it and says it's not true,
It's something I know I can prove.
For instance when tired after working all day,
And your bum hovers over a chair,
And the voice from the kitchen yells don't sit down yet,
Why it's more than the system can bear.

Then, when you're relaxing on some summer night,
And just contemplating a beer,
A voice says you've already had one of those,
You don't need another my dear.
When your eye catches sight of a beautiful girl
And you might risk a quick second glance,
Your ear hears a whisper that says, no you don't
Forget it, you haven't a chance.

And if I might think I'll go fishing,
Just get up and go with the dawn
The wife says, I'm sure you'll enjoy the day out
But, before you go please cut the lawn.
I'm sure that the womans' clairvoyant
It's enough to make a man weep,
I quite sure she knows what I'm dreaming about,
Even though she appears fast asleep.

I'm told that all females are like it,
It's something that's bred in the bone,
The clairvoyant bit of their brain never sleeps,
Even when they're just sitting alone.
I think that I'll set up a website,
To see if it's truly world wide,
So that bachelors can get early warning
If they're thinking of taking a bride

But I think there is nothing us husbands can do,
We may struggle, but nothing will change.
I suppose we could try never thinking
Or trying to keep out of range.
What would happen I wondered if I just left home,
But even then there was a snag,
For when I got home to tell my dear wife
I found out she was packing my bag.

My SatNav sweetheart.

I think I'll get rid of the missus
Yeah, I'll give the old menace the boot,
Because, when we go for a jaunt in the car
She can never give me the right route.
So I told her I'm going to change things,
Buy a SatNav to show us the way,
But the voice that I heard when I turned the thing on
Stole my heart when it started to play.

Yes, I'm in love with the girl in my SatNav,
It's quite true and I'm all of a dither,
And when she says turn right up some country lane
It sets my moustache all aquiver.
Now, I know some will say that my girl isn't real
That I'm dreaming my lifetime away,
But I can't resist when she whispers come on,
Now you're mine for the rest of the day.

And when every morning I jump in the car,
I know she'll be waiting to say,
Well darling and what was it took you so long,
Now, where can I take you today.
Then, off we will go over valley and hill,
Her seductive voice soft in my ear,
But, when she says slow down impetuous boy,
I must say I shed a small tear..

For I know we can never be truly as one,
That she'll go at the turn of a key,
That she's fickle, and when someone else drives the car
She'll no longer thinking of me.
But, for now I will follow wherever she leads
And continue to give her my heart,
And trust me and my girl in my SatNav
Stay together till death us do part.

A Good Day

Today I walked among the stars,
Touched Heaven with a glance,
Feel love possess me through and through,
Life swamp me with an urge
To hold it close, safe in my hand.

What brought about this state of grace,
Was this some aberration of the mind,
Some figment of imagination or
A dream perhaps or yet
Reality, either harsh or kind.

It was the latter, a wondrous gift,
A precious thing my heart beguiled,
Given with innocent, open heart,
Something to cherish my whole life long,
The smiliest smile of my small child.

Christmas

A hundred million stars tonight
Stand waiting in a winter sky,
For one great star who shines supreme,
A star to save us if we try
To heed it's light, sent here to say
To us is born a child today.

A light that some will never see,
Their eyes are blinded by the gleam
Of tinsel, glitter, twinkling lights.
For them Christmas has never been,
For Christmas is a story they will never understand,
Of how a simple family held a saviour in their hand.

But children hear the story
As they gather round a stall,
And see the simple crib within,
No comfort here at all.
Then every child goes back in time
To Bethlehem in Palestine.

To hear and say the simple words,
And join the oxen and the kings,
The shepherds as their watch they keep
And hear the song the angel sings,
To hear again the message clear
And know that Christmas time is near.

So let us celebrate this time
Of hope for peace on earth,
And listen to the message
Given in the virgin birth.
That man should dwell with man in peace
And strife and conflict now should cease.

Potty poems for Children

Adam Ant

On September 26th Adam Ant
went to the insect Post Office
to pay his road tax, only to find
10000 of his fellow ants in the
queue. This made him rather
cross, but he decided to wait a
little while.

Glancing round he spotted Alfie
the Anteater also in the queue,
and thought to himself that it was
time he went home to tea.

He went out shopping a couple
of days later and was surprised
to see how many ant roadster
cars there were for sale in the
car showrooms.

Alfie was seen to have a happy
smile on his face.

Ethel the Elephant

Ethel the Elephant
stood on a chair in the
bedroom, putting up
the curtains.

A fly landed on her
trunk making her jump.
she fell with a great
BANG!!!!!!!!

She went through the
ceiling, and fell on to
the table where Fred
was having his breakfast.

Fred spilled his tea and
swallowed his egg in
one bite. He was very
startled.

Ethel also fell onto the
fly who had caused all
the trouble. The fly did
not have a good day.

George

My name is George
I am a Giraffe.
A friend of mine
who scribbles a bit
asked me to give you
an insight into my
daily life, which was
nice of him.
So here goes.

I am extremely handsome,
my fur being a pleasant
brown in patches.
As you will be aware
I have a very long neck,
long legs (four) and a
short tail. My eyes and
ears are large and I have
two horn things on the
top of my head which
don't seem to do anything
except they are useful
for hanging hats on.

My long neck is an asset
when it comes to eating,
as I can reach to the tops
of trees and grab the best
leaves. I am a vegetarian,
not like those disgusting
Lions and Leopards, so this
is a definite advantage.
I can also beat that band
of thieving monkeys who
are always causing

Trouble.

It gets to be a problem
however when we go out
for a meal. There aren't
many restaurants or
burger bars with high
enough ceilings, and who
wants to sit outside in
Wintertime or when it rains.
You also have to sit a long
way from the table, which
takes up a lot of room,
which upsets some people.

The neck becomes a real
problem however when you
wish to travel. Imagine going
to visit an aged Aunt by car,
with your head poking out
of the side window.
It's very uncomfortable if
not dangerous, as your head
gets battered by the hedges

and if you meet a tree
the result can be a nasty
headache.
So, you say, go by bus.

Have you ever tried to get
on a bus carrying a ladder?
Say no more.

Aeroplanes are out, as one
gets rather breathless when
flying three miles up with
ones head stuck out of the
door. The driver gets
unhappy too at this
arrangement and the other
passengers get rather restless

That leaves travelling by
boat, but you don't see many
of those in the middle of Africa.
All in all travel is best not
bothered with. My long legs,
on the other hand, are very
useful. I can run very fast
when I have a lion or some
other nasty beast after me
and, if necessary, I can give
a very hard kick with my
big feet.

Some people say that my
legs look rather thin, but
I think they are rather elegant.
My tail is quite small and is
only good for waggling about
now and then. I also find it
useful, as, when it waggles
very fast I know it's going to rain.
I think that's all about me, and
it's time I took a stroll with the
family. So cheerio for now.
Take care.

The Plinky Plonky Bird

I met a man the other day
Who said that he had heard
That someone had discovered
A Plinky Plonky bird.

A large bird, a strange bird,
With multicoloured feather
Who always had to have his tea
Outside in any weather.

He has a great big yellow beak,
A tail some three feet long,
And if you treat him kindly
He'll sing for you a song.

He only sleeps whilst upside down
And has enormous feet,
And if you cook him egg and chips
He'll think it such a treat.

'A Plinky Plonky bird', he said
Appears but once a year
And only when the moon is full
And Christmas time is near.

Now, if you'd like to see this bird
He will be back quite soon,
He's been to see his Grandma
Who's living on the moon

Henrietta's Party

The plumes on his head fluttered gaily and bright,
His step it was firm and his eye had a glitter
A fine looking chap with a confident air,
That sent all his lady friends all of a twitter.
In a voice loud and clear which went echoing round
He said, 'Now my darlings come hither to me,
At once, if you please, I have something to say
Which I want you to ponder whilst having your tea.'
There was a great silence and then a commotion
As at once every hen without further ado
Started pushing and shoving and even stopped clucking
To hear every word and to get a good view.

'Now, you will remember' he said,' It's September,
Which means there's a birthday we should celebrate,
It's our Henrietta who's fifteen next Monday
We should have a party or even a fete.'
'Oh, lets have a party' the chickens all chorused,
'We could have a disco and nice things to eat,
Invite all the folks from the fields and the farmyard,
A splendid idea, it will be a treat'
'Very well' said the Cockerel,' A party it is then,
Send out invitations to friends one and all
To come to the barn at a quarter to midnight
And join all us chickens and we'll have a ball.'

The news of the party soon spread far and wide,
And everyone thought the idea was grand,
Wallace the Weasel said he'd bring his music
While Cedric the sheep said he'd make up a band.
Billy Goat played the trombone, the Turkey, the drums,
Percy Pig brought his trumpet, Fred Duck his guitar,
Sandy Stoat played piano, the Cat brought her fiddle
And everyone said it's the best band by far.
With the greatest excitement and anticipation,

They all fluffed their feathers and tidied their hair,
And even the Hedgehog had polished his bristles
It was going to be a most splendid affair.

On the night of the party, oh what great confusion
As everyone tried to find room for a dance,
'I'm certain' said Henry the horse to his partner
'There's so many people I shan't have a chance.'
Then, up on a bale of hay jumped the old Cockerel,
'Your attention,' he shouted, ' I won't keep you long,
There is something we mustn't forget before starting
Henrietta step forward, it's time for a song.

They played Happy Birthday and everyone sang,
The Owl said 'I don't think I've heard such a din
Since Matilda the Cow caught her tail in the tractor,'
The Cockerel said 'Right, let the party begin.'
Oh! What can be said of that wonderful party,
The singing, the dancing, the laughter the cheers,
'I think I can say' said the Bull to the Gander
'This party's the finest I've been to in years.'

THEN ON THE BARN DOOR CAME A
THUNDEROUS KNOCKING
Which made every creature there quiver with fear,
Then open the door flew and there stood the FARMER
Who said, very crossly 'WHAT'S GOIN' ON ' ERE.
Who said that you lot could have a big party,
It's two in the morning and we're all awake.
If you think that I'll let you keep on with this racket
Then I'm very afraid that you've made a mistake.'

Then up stepped the Cockerel all haughty and proud,
'Now just wait a moment and listen' he said,
'It's our Henrietta who's having a birthday
Now why don't you join us and not stay in bed.
You see, if your hens cannot finish the party

And have to go home they'll be ever so cross
You might not get eggs till a quarter to Tuesday
And that really would be a terrible loss.'

'Oh well,' said the farmer, 'That makes a big difference
I really had no wish to spoil your big night,
So I'll join, if I may, in the grand celebrations,
I'm sure it will give me the greatest delight.'
Then everyone cheered and the band started playing,
The party was once again soon in full swing,
And so it went on till the night met the morning,
'It won't be long now that the bluebells will ring'

Said the ram to a chicken 'It's time we were going.'
'Well then' said the Cockerel 'It's perfectly clear
We've had a great party so I've just decided
We must have another one this time next year.'
The animals thought this a splendid idea,
The farmer said he'd provide food for them all,
Why don't we invite everyone said the Badger.
If you'd like to be there then give me a call

Chickens of the world unite.!!!!!!!!

135

The Thrush and the Blackbird

A Thrush and a Blackbird sat up on a branch
Laughing and neighbourly talking
When they suddenly spotted right under their beaks A
worm, who was just going walking.

I say, said the Blackbird, just look at that worm
I could do with a bit of a meal.
And me, said the Thrush who was feeling quite faint
I must say it has it's appeal.

So down they both flew and examined the worm
Then looked at each other and said,
Let's toss to see which of us starts with the tail
While the other one tackles the head.

At this the poor worm who was rather afraid
That he wouldn't get home for his tea
Said, I say there you fellows that's not very nice
Have you bothered to think about me?

Why no, said the Blackbird, and no said the Thrush
You have taken us quite by surprise
For we always have worms to eat with our chips
And they make most delectable pies.

But if one of you start with my tail, said the worm
And one with my head, here's a riddle,
What's going to happen, oh please tell me, do,
When you meet head to head in the middle.

The Thrush and the Blackbird now thought hard and long
And the Thrush said, now here's a to-do
We're both now completely bamboozled
We'll have to think this thing right through.

Just imagine this happening time after time
Said the Blackbird quite shaken with shock,
My mates will turn white with the worry
And I'll be drummed out of the flock.

Well now, said the worm, I'm a fair minded chap
And hate to see you both worried
So I'll dash off home and ask my dear wife,
And off to his wormhole he scurried.

The Thrush and the Blackbird sat up on a branch
And whistled and trilled all day long,
They waited and waited till gone supper time
Said the Thrush, I'm sure something is wrong.

Look here said the Blackbird, I think we've been tricked
I knew we should never have tarried,
For I've just remembered the Owl told me once
That worms never, never get married.

What a swiz said the Thrush, I would never have guessed
It's a truly remarkable tale
I think we should try and forget the whole thing
And instead find a big juicy snail.

And what of the worm as he sat in his hole
And sampled his lovely cream tea,
I must be more careful when dealing with birds,
At least that is what he told me.

The Little Man

One day I met a little man
A sitting on a stair.
I said, 'My dear old Fellow
What funny clothes you wear'

His coat was red, his hat was blue
With multicoloured hose.
He had a silver shilling
Which he balanced on his nose.

'The clothes I wear my dear young Sir'
He said 'Are very fine,
The cloth was spun by silkworms
At the bottom of a mine.

The buttons shining on the coat
Were made by ogres three
The metal it is fairy gold,
They make them just for me'.

'But why, my dear old Fellow
Do you sit upon this stair,
And why the shilling on the nose,
Did you do it for a dare'

'Oh no, my dear young Sir,' he said
'I started very small,
I think it was a horse and cart,
Why, nothing large at all.'

'I'm sitting here,' he said to me
'Until it's time for tea
And if you'd care to come along
You can share it for a fee.

I'll only charge you fifty pence
Which really is quite cheap,
There's currant buns and jelly
Which I make while I'm asleep.

There's also hedgehog sandwiches
And jam I've made from snails,
And winkles from a winkle farm
Brought to me by whales.'

I said to him, 'You're very odd
You get me in a muddle,'
So I simply raised my hat to him
And pushed him in a puddle.

The Tail of Maurice

Maurice the Mouse
Crossed the road

A lorry came
Very very fast

It ran over
His tail.

Wheeeeeeeee!
He now has

The longest
And flattest

Tail in the whole
WORLD.

Sidney the Seagull

Sidney the Seagull stood on a rock,
On one leg, looking at the sea,
A gust of wind blew suddenly
And over he went, webbed feet over
beak, straight into a rock pool.
He got very wet and cross.

He also felt very silly, as seagulls
are not supposed to get blown
off a rock and into a rock pool.
So he jumped quickly back on to
the rock and tried to look as
though nothing had happened.

Unfortunately, a passing cockle
had seen the whole thing and,
as cockles are usually eaten by
Seagulls, he was very amused and
shouted 'Hey there Sidney, have
you been drinking again'.

He then ducked down behind a rock.
Just to be on the safe side.
Sidney searched everywhere, but
couldn't find the cockle and so he
he flew home for his tea, which was
his favourite, squid with a seaweed sauce.

The following morning Sarah, his wife,
sent Sidney to the beach to get a copy
of the Seaside Gazette, which they
could read while having their breakfast
of winkles on toast with custard.

He was a very happy seagull but then.
He was suddenly aware that something
was very odd indeed. Everyone was
smiling and nodding, and a group of
young cockles burst into giggles,
while a passing starfish laughed very
loudly. It got odder and odder.

The cormorant selling the papers gave
him a wink and a chuckle and said,
' Fallen into any good rock pools lately'
This was too much and he suddenly
felt a trickle of apprehension running
through him. Someone had talked.

He grabbed the paper and scuttled away
to a secluded part of the beach where he
opened it and saw, horrors upon horrors,
his own face staring back at him
He saw the beady eye, the beak,
and knew he was in trouble.

His feathers stood on end.
He twitched, he trembled.
He thought, what will I do.
Should I throw myself off a cliff
and forget to open my wings.
What will Sarah say.

A shadow fell upon the sand.
' Well, well, if it isn't Sidney' a
voice said. It was Henry, the
King of the beaches, a very large
Seagull. 'You have made us seagulls
look very silly haven't you', he said,

'Everyone will think that we can't
stand on one leg without falling
over'. 'I think you should put that
right by standing on one leg on top
of the lighthouse for a week to show
that you can do it, don't you'.

'Oh yes Sir, right away Sir, at once
Sir' said Sidney, glad to get away, and
off he flew to start standing on one leg
on top of the lighthouse. But, do you
know, he still falls over now and then.
It's very odd.

So the next time you are at the
Seaside and see a seagull standing
on one leg, it will be Sidney, and if
he falls over, do pick him up, dust off
the sand, and stand him up again, please.
He will appreciate it.

Hi there Sidney!!!

The Christmas Cake

One Christmas Eve a strange young man
who wore a top hat painted green
said to a baker can you make
the biggest cake you've ever seen.
It must be tall as my top hat,
the roundest thing that there could be,
quite full of lovely things to eat,
with icing sweet as sweet can be.

I'll pay you well with golden dreams,
you'll be as famous as can be
and everyone will know your name
if you will bake this cake for me.
But I must have it made tonight,
and to be sure that you'd succeed
I'll get a friend of mine to send
all the help that you might need.

The baker said "I'll do my best
so lets get started right away."
The young man waved a hand and said
"there now your help is on the way"
At once there came a rush of wind,
and then a pattering and a clattering,
and skipping through the doorway came
a crowd of pixies happily chattering.

They all wore pointed hats of green
with coats of brown and pink and blue,
with buttons made of fairy gold
and trousers in a scarlet hue.
Each carried spoons to stir the mix
of flour and lots of fruit and spice
and bags of sugar came behind
in tiny wagons pulled by mice.

"Right" said the baker "off we go"
and all the pixies joined the fun
stirring and mixing, and mixing and stirring
busily working until it was done.
Then, into the oven the cake was put,
and while it was baking they all had tea
of fairy cakes, lemonade made from dew
and sandwiches picked from a cucumber tree.

Then when at last the cake was baked
they took it from the oven with care
for, after all the work they'd done
to spoil it now they didn't dare.
and, while it cooled their spoons they took
to make the icing sweet and white,
"Oh hurry do" the young man said
"it must be finished for tonight".

So faster still the pixies worked
to make the icing for the cake,
and then at last the baker said
"you've made enough and now lets take
it to the cake, and with my knife
I'll spread it quickly thick and smooth
and then at last it's nearly done.
I'm sure the young man will approve".

"Indeed I do" the young man said
"But still there's one thing to be done,
we must have candles for the top"
Hooray, Hooray, cried everyone.
The baker said "I've got some here,
I'll go and get them from my store".
Away he rushed and very soon
returned with hundreds, maybe more.

The pixies took a candle each
and quickly put them into place,
"That's excellent" the young man said
which brought a smile to every face.
The baker wasn't quite so pleased,
"There's one small thing I can't ignore",
he said "Will someone tell me please
just who this Christmas cake is for".

"It's made for Santa Claus of course",
the young man said, and all his elves,
"because they haven't got the time
to bake a cake just for themselves".
"How splendid" cried the baker," but
although the thought is very nice
how can you take a cake this big
to the land of snow and ice".

"That's quickly done", the young man said
"for if I raise my hat you see,
my friend the fairy Queen will send
all her subjects here to me
and they will lift our cake with ease
and in an instant off they fly.
They'll be with Santa and his elves
in the twinkling of an eye".

And so it was, and right away
the air was filled with specks of light
as all the fairies fluttered down.
It really was a wondrous sight.
Then in a flash the cake was gone.
"Now we must hurry off, I fear",
the young man said "but don't be sad,
for we'll be back again next year".

The Insect Olympics

I'm **IN** for the Insect Olympics
I'm jumping for England at last,
they gave me the invite this morning,
so now all the worry is past.

I don't think I'll let down the country,
my leap is exceedingly long,
my legs are just bulging with muscle,
I can't see how I can go wrong.

I know that I shan't be the favourite,
no Grasshopper ever has won,
the Frogs have been training for ages,
while we've just been jumping for fun.

The last time a Grasshopper entered
it must have been four years ago,
he ended up last of the jumpers,
it gave us a terrible blow.

But I think that someone should enter,
us Grasshoppers never give in
and it's time that the Frogs had a beating,
as I'm sure that I'm going to win.

My Coach says my training is over,
I'm physically right at my peak
my jumping technique now is flawless.
The reason is not far to seek.

My Coach was a champion leaper,
a Bullfrog of greatest renown,
he won the Olympics a record four times,
as well as the Commonwealth crown.

It really is very exciting,
it's held in Geneva this year,
they say that the entry's enormous,
but we Brits have nothing to fear.

Our team is just oozing with talent
The Beetles and Fleas are the best
in the field sports, and high jump and pole vault,
while Spiders will outrun the rest.

We're flying out Saturday morning,
the birds are arranging the flight,
but mixing up birds and us insects,
well somehow it doesn't seem right.

But still, it will be an adventure
and everyone wants to be there,
to carry the flag for Great Britain,
and join in this glorious affair.

So give a big cheer for us insects,
as off to the Games we all fly,
I'm sure that we'll win lots of medals,
so lets go and give it a try.

The Invitation

The Crocodile to the Warthog said
You're very pretty, shall we wed,
or maybe dance a jig or two,
or paint each other's foreheads blue

Well now, the Warthog said, I fear
I really have no time my dear,
and furthermore I've heard it said
your dancing partners end up dead.

Then come to lunch you lovely girl
you should be giving life a whirl,
I'm sure you'll like my toast and jam
it goes quite well with chips and ham.

Then after lunch we'll take a stroll,
I know a lovely muddy hole
where we can sleep the day away,
I'll sing a love song if I may.

The Warthog said, how very sweet
I'm sure that it will be a treat,
and all that mud sounds very nice,
a love song also does entice.

But somehow, when I see the gleam
of all those teeth it seems a dream
and though you smile it's plain to see
that you would like me for your tea.

So thank you for the invitation,
This news will please the Warthog nation,
That crocs are such a gentle bunch
so long as you don't stay to lunch.

The Old Man

When I was young, the old man said,
I never, ever went to bed.

I used to try and make pigs sneeze,
Or sit with sparrows in the trees.

I sometimes played with polar bears
Or dined with tigers in their lairs.

I swam with dolphins in the sea
Invited fairy's home to tea.

Went dancing with a crocodile
And tickled trout to make them smile.

And though I'm getting old and grey
I still find time to laugh and play.

I've been invited by a frog
To join him in his murky bog.

I wish you'd join me said a king
I'm off to hear a walrus sing.

It therefore seems to me, it's plain
I'll have to start it all again.

The Sparrow and the Pig

'Why is your tail so curly'
Said a Sparrow to a Pig,
'And why your ears so very large,
And why your nose so big'.

The Pig said 'You are very rude,
And think you're very smart,
But we Pigs have a secret,
Which sets us quite apart'.

'You're not the only ones you know
 to gambol in the sky,
Although we've kept it hidden,
we pigs, you know, can fly..

'Ho, Ho, Ha, Ha' the Sparrow laughed
'That's really quite absurd
It's just about the biggest joke
That I have ever heard'.

'Oh really!' said the angry Pig
' Now listen here to me
You flap your tiny wings to fly
We flap our ears you see'.

'My nose is what we follow,
When flying high and free,
And when our curly tails go straight
We know it's time for tea.'

'But you're so big' the Sparrow said
I can't believe it's true'
The Pig then simply flapped his ears
And off to tea he flew.

The Watcher

I'm sitting, watching, on this hill.
They say I'm bound to get a thrill,

Because an old man said that I
Will see a cabbage flying by

Provided that I wait a bit.
I can't miss that so here I sit.

What sort it is there is some doubt,
I'm hoping it's a Brussels sprout.

But if it's not I'll get great joy
If it's a Broccoli or Savoy.

He also said that every noon
Or sometimes, when there is a moon,

An onion or a runner bean
Or even courgettes can be seen

All sailing gently through the air,
But cucumbers are very rare.

He said one evening in July
He saw a lettuce floating by.

A parsnip then went slowly past
and then a radish, rather fast.

But most of all, a great sensation,
A bunch of carrots in formation.

I'd love to see these wondrous things,
Like beans and cabbages with wings.

So here I am, and here I stay,
I just can't take my eyes away.

Herewith
a couple of
monologues

A Wedding and that.

There was a wedding in our village a couple of weeks ago -- in the church -- church of England that is.

It could've been any of the others.

There's the Baptists -- they shoves you under water afore they allows you to join.

Sommat to do with Jesus being ducked in a river by one of 'is mates.

It wouldn't do for me though -- we only washed all over but once a year -- at Easter. Arr'

All the family -- all twelve of us, one after the other -- starting with Dad, then Mum and so on

----except the twins -- they goes in together.

Mum topped us up with a kettle.

I still keeps up the tradition -- though now I've changed it to Whit Monday.

The rest of the year we just let's it flake off -- well I mean -- taters don't get washed all over --it

just falls off when it's dry.

I meets the vicars wife one time.

She starts off straight away.

You smells she says -- you smells somethin' 'orible she says.

Why don't you wash, she says, you smells, she says.

Well missus, I says, I will if you promises to wash my back I says.

That 'ad 'er, -- she goes pink and off she goes.

I wonder if she washes the vicars back. Ha'.

Then there's the Primitive Methodists, the Weslions and the Spiritulists -- they be in a corrugated

shed -- up by the railway.

I never seed anybody go'in in there -- nor comin' out -- maybe they just turns into spirits and disappears. Hah.

One time Jimmy 'awkins goes up there to see if 'e could see is missus who 'ad just died.

We don't know w'ot 'e found out but 'e left for Orstratia soon 'ater. -- she 'ad a sharp tongue or 'er she did. She could cut a two inch plank with it.

I went to the wedding -- well I was leanin' on the wall -- by the lych gate -- on account that I'd just come from the Rose 'an Crown.

The first to arrive was Miss Beckett who plays the organ.

I can't abide 'er. Always finding fault she was.

She'd go terrin' about the village on 'er tricycle poking 'er nose into everythin'.

I seed you she said. I seed you. You bin down to that den of iniquity she says -- the Rose 'an Crown -- you 'av bin participatin' of the juice of the apple she said -- like Adam and Eve --

The book of Genesis, she says.

Very big on words she was -- not that I understood many of 'em o' course.

Well, says I, is wot they got up to by drinkin' the juice of the apple the same as wot you an' the Vicar gets up to, drinkin' that bottle o' sacrificial wine of a Friday ev'nin' while choosin' the Sunday hymns, I says.

That stopped 'er. I never seed anybody run into the church so fast. She al'us 'ad a smile on 'er face on a Saturday though. Hah.

Our church is not very big. It's got a lot of them memorials stuck on the wall, so that if they come back, they know they're in the right place. Har.

Nearly all the village turned up -- the verger was nearly trampled underfoot.

Old Mrs Watkins cleared a bit of space with 'er zimmer frame -- you should have 'eard the language -- and that was just Mrs Watkins. I never knew she knew words like that -- and 'er a good churchgoer too.

Any'ow they all crammed in and waited for the bride to be.

All in white she was, which was a bit of a surprise, seein' what 'er and our Billy got up to in the barn that time -- maybe she 'ad a bit of mauve somewhere.

Still -- it were a nice weddin'.

I went back to the Rose 'an Crown an' raised a pint to the bridegroom -- 'e was goin' to need all the 'elp 'e could get later on I 'spect.

Got to go now. Ta Ta.

Old Charlie

I 'ad an 'air cut last week. Well, it were time as I 'as one every six month or so.

The barber says its more like shearin' than 'aircutting, an then 'e charges me ten shilling's.

I says I can get a sheep sheared for five shillings. Right 'e says, get your clothes off 'e says 'an I'll start at the bottom 'an work my way up 'e says, like a sheep.

I went a bit quiet 'ater that.

Mind you 'e only knows short back 'an sides 'an puddin' basin for boys. 'is speciality is shavin'.

The old boys 'as the full treatment, including' the red 'ot towels. They comes out lookin' like red billiard balls.

When the vicar first come to the village 'e comes in for a shave, sits in the chair 'an gets all lathered up.

The barber stropps his razor and goes behind 'im to start, when the vicar leaps out of the seat yellin', you aint going to shave me from the back, 'e yells -- you shave me from the front 'e yells, or not at all.

Well, o' course, the barber didn't know whether the vicar mistook 'im for Sweeny Todd or whether there was som'at agin it in the Bible, such as Thou shalt not cut a

vicar's throat with a razor or some such. Hah.

Anyhow 'e managed somehow, though I daresay the vicar did a lot o' prayin' an' the barbers 'and shook a bit too.

Now, some folk don't like sharp tools. Like Charlie Bevan. 'es out toppin' swedes one time up in Farmer Smiths top field, an' 'e takes off two fingers as sweet as you like. 'e reckoned 'e lost 'undreds of pounds 'cos 'e counted up on 'is fingers like the rest of us an' he was always two pounds less in 'is wages than us.

'e never worked it out.

'e kept 'is fingers in a little tin and used 'em to frighten the kids.

'e showed them to old Martha Evans once.

She 'it 'im with 'er umbrella, then whips out 'er glass eye and laughs at Charlie,

Beat that then she says. That slowed old Charlie down a bit.

Mind you, old Charlie used to get around a bit when 'e were a young lad. We 'ad a new schoolmaster up at the school and 'e says, I can't understand it 'e says, I can't understand it. Nearly all the children in this village looks the same e' says.

I could 'av told 'im. Charlie knew 'is onions from 'is beetroot as many of the ladies in the village could testify.

'e was a good gardener and one year 'is cucumbers was the biggest in the flower an' veg show, which raised a smile from some of the ladies as they passed by.

'e died last week an' the Womens Institute want to put up a monument to Charlie. Fancy that, a monument for enjoyin' yourself. Ah well.

Got to go now.

The Cricket Match

We 'ad a cricket match in the village last week. Our village against Nether Dewchurch for the sparagrass cup.

It's bin goin' on for 'undreds of years they say, 'undreds. In fact the vicar reckons that the Saxons played the Normans up on the top field, some argiment about who's turn it was to do the mow'in on the glebe fields, 'e says.

Any'ow it's very old and 'as led to some fine battles.

This is because Nether Dewchurch usually wins and we 'and't 'eld the cup for many years. Since the turn of the century they reckons. Har..

The trouble is Squire Belmont who's Dewchurch's team captain. E's got to play cause 'e owns the field, and if 'e don't play neither does anybody else.

We've only got the vicar, and 'es captain because 'es the only one in the village with a pair of white cricket trousers and proper boots. Our lads wears their hobnails.

The main problem we 'as, is that the squire invites some of 'is mates to join in and one or two of 'em 'av been right ringers (that is, they 'av played for big teams and are good- but the squire don't tell us that).

Not only that, but the blacksmith also plays for them, and 'es a right villain, in fact we reckons 'e is an omicidal maniac when it comes to cricket--'es sent more lads from our village to the orspital with shellshock than ever came out of the war.

All we got is John Wards boy Cecil, 'oos a nice lad but a bit delicut like and fritens

easy, 'an John Bloggs the village bobby 'oo puts the frighteners on the opposition 'cus if they don't let 'im score a few runs thay'm likely to end up inside for the night whether they 'av done anything or no.

Anyhow, the two umpires goes to the wicket in their white coats, borrowed from

Mr Smith the butcher and tosses a coin, which is a double 'eaded shillin' which they uses every year an' which we all knows about.

The Squire yells 'ed as usual, and puts 'is team in to bat.

Our opening bowlers were John Ward's boy Cecil and Edward Machen the bank manager, who is as artful as a bag of monkeys.

The very first ball had the Squire leg before wicket, as plain as a pikestaff, but the Squire refused to go off.

They've come to see me 'e yelled, not some beardless boy 'e yelled. I'm not going,

I'm not out 'e yelled.

Then the two umpires got involved, our's sayin' you're out, and the other sayin, the opposite.

Things got a bit heated and it finished up with a fight with a stump each. Very entertainin' it were.

It were sorted out by Enid Green from the sweet shop 'oo ran onto the pitch an' set about 'em both with 'er walking stick. Quick on 'er feet is Enid.

It sort of settled down after that, and we started to take a wicket or two, and they started to make a few runs and by tea time they 'ad made sixty all out and everybody went off to 'ave cucumber sandwiches an' some rock cakes made by the vicar's wife which you could break a tooth on.

Then it were our turn to bat and Joe Brent went in first. 'e 'ad to be paid o' course 'an 'e made sure 'e 'ad plenty of insurance. But even then 'e were as white as a sheet

'an you could see 'im trembling' from the bar of the Rose 'an Crown.

This were 'cus the Squire gave the ball to the blacksmith to open the bowling 'an 'e smiled at Joe in a very nasty way - you know, all teeth 'an chuckle.

He walked right back to the boundary to begin 'is run up but then kept on goin', past the sight screen and into the long grass, until 'e were out 'o sight.

The first thing Joe saw were the top of 'is 'ed as 'e appeared 'an then the rest of 'im

getting' faster 'an faster, like a train leavin' a station.

'e reached the wicket, leapt in the air 'an 'urled the ball at Joe.

Nobody saw where it 'ad gone but we 'eard the crash as it took a piece out 'o the far sightscreen. Joe fell to the ground with a scream 'an covered 'is 'ed with 'is 'ands.

'e were led gently away to the beer tent mutterin' to his self "why me, why me, what 'av I done".

The next man in were the vicar 'oo dropped to 'is knees 'an prayed for divine assistance - but it were no good, the blacksmith would 'av put the wind up the Archbishop Gabriel.

The next one threw down 'is bat 'an ran for it while the next two 'ad to be drugged with cider and led to the wicket, but it didn't 'elp. The situation were desprit, five wickets down for no runs.

On the last ball of the over the blacksmith were enjoyin' 'iself, but, as 'e got to the

wicket and leapt to deliver the ball a voice from the

crowd yelled "I knows who you was in the barn with last Saturday "

That were when something very funny 'appened.

As 'e were flyin' through the air with a smile on 'is face, all 'is joints seem to 'av come undone somehow 'an 'e landed in a cloud 'o dust at midwicket, on 'is 'ed.

There was complete silence all the way round the ground and then the batsman went up 'an kicked 'im to see if 'e were alive.

'e was carried off to the bar of the beer tent to see if a pint of cider would 'elp, but 'e

couldn't continue to play to our lads relief.

I suppose, in a way, we were a bit sorry for 'im 'cus we 'ad 'eard that 'is missus 'ad

threatened to remove 'is weddin' tackle if 'e were caught again with that

Gloria Wilkins. She were very fierce were 'is missus.

It didn't make much difference though, and we didn't score any more runs.

But then John Boggs the bobby went in to bat, an' we 'ad 'igh 'opes of 'im.

'e was always a bit impatient were John, an' 'e straight away took a mighty swipe and

the ball went off the edge of the bat, straight up in the air an' into some long grass that

'ad been left just inside the boundary by Farmer Smith when 'e mowed the field.

Staight away all the Dewchurch lads rushed over to find it, whilst our lads ran as fast as they could to make as many runs as possible before the ball was found.

That grass was very long and our lads had made fiftynine runs afore they found it, and, by then, John Bloggs the bobby were exhausted 'an 'ad to retire.

Well, we thought, that were it 'an we 'ad lost again, when the vicar yelled, "Just a minute, we've bin playin' this 'ere match with ten men not eleven, so we're one short,

there's one more to come."

So, a count was made, 'an 'e were quite right, there was only ten men on our side, but I 'ad seen Willy Smart creepin' off to get 'is milkin' done early 'cus 'e were doin' a bit 'o courting' 'an 'is Betty was a bit reluctant like 'an 'e needed a bit more time to change 'er mind.

But I didn't say nothing.

Everythin' 'ad gone very quiet, 'an I suddenly realised they was all looking at me.

"You can go in" says the vicar, "you've been doin' all the shoutin' 'an we only want you to make two runs, you can go in 'e yells".

Well, I'd 'ad a couple of ciders at the beer tent, so I wasn't in any condition to argue, so they gives me a bat 'an pushed me onto the wicket.

The bowler was the Squire 'an we didn't like one another, on account that I 'ad beat 'im at the flower show, my roses bein' better than 'is.

Right, 'e says, superior like, try this for size, and bowled the ball.

It were the cider I suppose, but I saw two balls comin' at me, so I 'it's the nearest.

I don't remember much ater that, but they tells me that I

'ad 'it that ball right out of the ground and into the bar of the Rose and Crown.

It 'it Sam Preedy the publican on the 'ed, 'an 'e were so surprised that as 'e fell to the floor 'e said "Drinks all round" 'an then fainted when 'e realised what 'e 'ad said.

Any way, we 'ad won 'an the vicar 'ad the church bells rung. 'e said in 'is sermon

that I 'ad been inspired by feelin's of patriotism 'an sacrifice, but I reckon that the cider 'ad somthin' to do with it. Don't you?.

So long for now.

The Ghost in the attic or a Christmas Tale.

The man stood looking over the extensive lawn which stretched away to a line of trees now quite bare of leaves because it was just four weeks to Christmastime.

He was tall and well dressed in a tweed suit that smacked of money, had hair beginning to grey at the temples, and carried an air of self satisfaction on his rather thin face.

He was feeling satisfied with life because he and his family had finally managed to get themselves settled into their new house in time for the festive season. They had moved to the village from the town and so knew few people as yet, but his wife was determined to find some of the friends and neighbours the family had been lacking in their old streets where people kept themselves to themselves and had little time for anyone else in their busy lives.

The man turned as there came a knock at the door and then a commotion as two children came dashing in.

'Steady on there' he said 'there's no need to run' as the children skidded to a stop.

'Sorry father' said the boy who was a well built lad of some twelve summers, which was echoed by his sister who was a couple of years younger but just as active as her brother.

The two had just arrived home from school and were like a couple of energetic puppies, wanting to explore everything and anything which moved or not in their new home.

"There's four boys coming up the drive" piped up his sister, "we'll go and see what they want", and off they ran. The children, whose names were George and Jenny, arrived at the door at the same time as the boys were about to ring the bell, and the two groups stood looking at one another.

"Hello," said George "What can we do for you?".

The oldest lad smiled and asked if their father was at home and if so could he have a word with him.

At that point their father arrived and enquired of the lads what it was they wanted and, in reply was given a small piece of paper which stated that the children of the village were being asked to give up a toy to be given to those children who had none and would receive none. They would be collected at the church the week before Christmas. The note was signed by the vicar.

"I'll have to think about this" said their father, "but I don't think that these two have any toys to spare, but if they have then I will let you know". He closed the door with a bang and muttered "the cheek of it", which didn't hold out much hope for the lads outside.

The next Sunday the family went to the local church where they were met and welcomed by the churchwarden and shown to a pew, right at the front under the pulpit.

The service went well except for an elderly man who looked slightly scruffy, sitting quite close in the same pew. He had long grey hair and wore a rather old fashioned coat which looked as though it had seen better days.

At the end of the service the vicar spoke to the family and the father introduced himself as John Bentley and then the rest of the family in turn, and then remarked to the vicar that the elderly man in the same pew didn't sing at all and seemed a little strange.

"That's very odd "said the vicar" as there was no one but you and the family in that pew, I can assure you"

"But there was" said John "see, he has left a key where he was sitting." The key was an old one and had appeared to have had a good deal of use and when John picked it up seemed to be slightly warm to the touch. "Well, how peculiar " said the vicar, "If you like I'll take the key and see if he comes back for it, if, of course he ever existed," but John for some reason felt that he should hold on to it and dropped it into his pocket.

In the next few days the children explored the entire house which was a very old rambling place, getting very dusty but pleased with themselves and, one evening when the family were sitting down to eat George remarked that they had found one room at the end of a corridor which was locked and which seemed to have someone in it because they could hear someone crying, and it sounded like a child.

"Well, that's nonsense " said their father "There is no way that anyone could be in this house without us noticing before now", "I'll go and look when we have finished and you can come with me and see how silly you are to say things like that".

And so a short time later they all trooped upstairs to the room and stopped outside the door and listened, and there it was, a child sobbing as though their heart was broken.

John Bentley stood with his mouth open, quite unable to take in what he was hearing; but then his wife broke the spell by saying that they had to get in and at once and see who it was.

But they had no key, but suddenly John thought of the key left by the old man in church, and later he was to wonder how the thought had popped into his mind at this time and not at any other.

"Go and get the key which you will find in my desk George, the right hand drawer"

"Quickly now".

George ran his fastest and soon returned with the old key, which his father quickly used to open the door, much to his surprise, because that was the last thing he expected would happen.

However, they all pressed into the room in some excitement, which was small with only one small window which had no curtains and was covered with grime. There was very little furniture, just a truckle bedstead in one corner, with no bedclothes, a table and chair, and all surfaces were covered with a layer of dust and cobwebs, giving the impression that the room had been kept closed for a long long time.

Everyone stood for some minutes feeling the strangeness of the room when Jenny blurted out "listen, the sobbing has stopped". It had.

They listened for a further fifteen minutes, but the room remained as silent as the grave, so everyone was ushered out and the door relocked the door, but, as they started to walk away the sobbing started again, the deep sobs of a child in distress.

The family was now alarmed and John Bentley decided to speak again with the old vicar, whom they were sure knew more than he was saying.

It was only after some pressure that the vicar told the story of the family who had lived in the house years before.

It seemed that there was a man, his wife and a young boy of about five who lived in the house, seemingly quite happily, but one day the boy had run into the road and in saving him the wife had been killed.

From then on the father became a recluse, the boy was taken from the local school and had private tutors and was never seen by anyone in the village, the story being that he had been sent to live with an aunt some distance away. A story many didn't believe.

The father eventually died, but there was never any sign of the lad, he had simply disappeared and, although there had been extensive enquiries nothing was ever found

And that is how the matter remained.

However, other people who had lived in the house had also heard the sobbing and gradually no-one would live there.

Now John Bentley knew why the house was relatively cheap to buy and was furious that no one had told him the full story.

Now, meanwhile, Jenny and George who had been greatly affected by what had happened, and being curious as most children are, had decided to go back for another look at the room and, after some discussion, had agreed to take a few of their toys to leave behind on the table, as it seemed to them that, if there was a child there, he had nothing to play with and sounded lonely and sad.

They took the key from their fathers desk, crept upstairs to the room and went in, being aware that, once again the sobbing had stopped.

They put the toys on the table and Jenny said out loud "We are sorry that you sound so sad and lonely, please play with the toys whoever you are".

They tiptoed quietly out and relocked the door, noticing that the sobbing had not restarted as it had before.

That evening their father announced that the vicar was coming to see what could be done, if anything, to get rid of the sobbing, which gave the children some concern that their parents would see the toys they had left, after being told that they mustn't go into the room again.

The following day the vicar arrived with bell, book and candle, said words of prayer in the room, the door was then locked, and he went away, saying that he had cured the sobbing, but that smething had been put on the table as the dust had been disturbed but that there was nothing there now.

As there as nothing to see, no-one took any notice at his remark, and the children didn't mention what they had done.

From then on no more sobbing was heard and, of course, the vicar took the credit but the children felt that they too had helped, and afterwards wondered how had the toys been moved for they were never found again.

John Bentley thought a great deal about what had happened to that poor, sad and lonely young soul in that attic room and determined to make this Christmas the very best he could for is own and other children. He became a changed man helping others and making sure that the lads who had come asking for toys for the poorer children had plenty to take away.

So everything ended happily for them all, but nothing was ever found out about the child in the small room at the end of the corridor. Perhaps he knew he was remembered and wasn't lonely any more.

Good night, sleep tight.

37976198R00098

Made in the USA
Charleston, SC
23 January 2015